D1266992

Out of HABIT

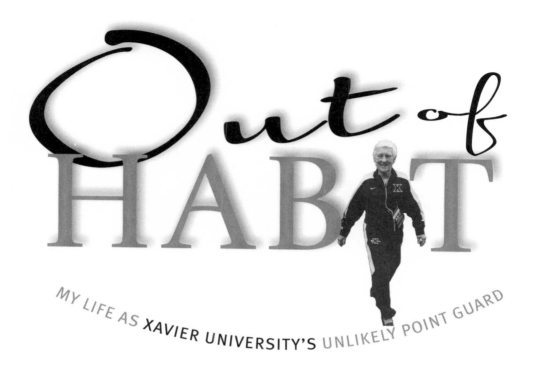

Out of HABIT

MY LIFE AS XAVIER UNIVERSITY'S UNLIKELY POINT GUARD

SISTER ROSE ANN FLEMING
with LAURA PULFER

ORANGE *frazer* PRESS
Wilmington, Ohio

ISBN 9781939710185
Copyright©2014 Xavier University

No part of this publication may be reproduced in any material form (including photocopying or storing
in any medium by electronic means and whether or not transiently or incidentally to some other use of
this publication) without the written permission of the copyright holder except in accordance with the
provisions of the Copyright, Designs and Patents Act 1988.

Published for Xavier University by:
Orange Frazer Press
P.O. Box 214
Wilmington, OH 45177
Telephone: 800.852.9332 for price and shipping information.
Website: *www.orangefrazer.com*
www.orangefrazercustombooks.com

Book and cover design: Brittany Lament and Orange Frazer Press

Cover photo by Greg Rust of the author with Dante Jackson in 2011.
Laura Pulfer photo by Kimberly Cline.

All proceeds from the sale of the book will go to the Sister Rose Ann Fleming Academic Advising
Endowment Fund to continue Sister's work for Xavier student athletes. For more information:
www.xavier.edu/outofhabit

Library of Congress Cataloging-in-Publication Data

Fleming, Rose Ann, 1935-
 Out of habit : my life as Xavier University's unlikely point guard / Sister Rose Ann Fleming with Laura
Pulfer.
   pages cm
 Includes index.
 ISBN 978-1-939710-18-5
 1. Fleming, Rose Ann, 1935- 2. Xavier University (Cincinnati, Ohio)--Faculty. 3. Faculty advisors--Ohio-
-Cincinnati. 4. Mentoring in education--Ohio--Cincinnati. 5. Xavier University (Cincinnati, Ohio)--
Basketball. 6. Basketball players--Counseling of. 7. Basketball players--Conduct of life. 8. Pulfer, Laura,
1946- I. Title.
 LD4852.8.F54A3 2014
 378'.040977178--dc23
                        2014030748

Printed in the United States of America
First printing

"The palest ink is more reliable than the most powerful memory."

—Confucius

To Linda and Bob Kohlhepp for the encouragement and the ink.
To my family, spiritual and corporal, and to the good God
who placed them in my path and who is with me in all things.

And for the incomparable, unique young men who taught me so much.
It gives me such joy to know that they are carrying the lessons we learned
together to every corner of the world and into the lives of all they touch.

Acknowledgments

Thanks to eagle-eyes Kelly Leon, Sister Jane Roberts, Rosie Hyden, Cynthia Hardie, Mike Pulfer and Jan Annett and to photographer Greg Rust. Tom Eiser's frighteningly encyclopedic memory of Xavier basketball was invaluable, as was the gentle prodding of Trustee Kay Napier and wise counsel of John Kucia. Sisters Louanna Orth and Mary Ann Barnhorn, provided sage historical perspective, and Bobbie Terlau was our cyberspace navigator.

—Sister Rose Ann Fleming

Gratitude and love to: Andy Donnelly, Richie Harris, Eddie Johnson, John Kelley, Ralph Lee, Walt McBride (Senior season, 1985-1986); J.D. Barnett, Dexter Campbell, Byron Larkin, Walt Corbean (1987-1988); Stan Kimbrough, Mike Ramey (1988-1989); Tyrone Hill, Derek Strong, Jerry Butler, Bob Koester (1989-1990); Michael Davenport, Colin Parker, Jamal Walker (1990-1991); Chris Mack (1991-1992); Aaron Williams, Jamie Gladden, Eric Knop, Mark Poynter, Dwayne Wilson (1992-1993); Brian Grant, Erik Edwards, Steve Gentry, Tyrice Walker (1993-1994); Michael Hawkins, Larry Sykes, Jeff Massey, DeWaun Rose, Pete Sears (1994-1995); Mark Smydra (1995-1996); Sherwin Anderson, Kevin Carr, Ken Harvey, Jim Kromer (1996-1997); Torraye Braggs, T.J. Johnson, Pat Kelsey, Matt Terpening (1997-1998); James Posey, Lenny Brown, Gary Lumpkin, Darnell Williams (1998-1999); Obi Harris (1999-2000); Reggie Butler, Marcus Mason, Maurice McAfee (2000-2001); James Baronas, Alvin Brown, Kevin Frey (2001-2002); David West, Ryan Caldwell, Lionel Chalmers (2002-2003); Tom Compton, Romain Sato, Anthony Myles (2003-2004); Keith Jackson (2004-2005); Brandon Cole, Dedrick Finn, Keenan Christiansen, Will Caudle, Brian Thornton (2005-2006); Justin Doellman, Justin Cage, Adam Simons, Kevin Waymire (2006-2007); Stanley Burrell, Josh Duncan, Drew Lavender (2007-2008); Derrick Brown, C.J. Anderson, B.J. Raymond (2008-2009); Jason Love (2009-2010); Kevin Feeney, Joe Hughes, Danté Jackson, Johnny Mazza, Jamel McLean, Andrew Taylor (2010-2011); Brad Redford, Travis Taylor, Mark Lyons, Tu Holloway, Kenny Frease (2011-2012); Jeff Robinson, Isaiah Philmore, Erik Stenger (2012-2013); Matt Stainbrook, Justin Martin, Tim Whelan (2013-2014).

Foreword

I have never known Xavier University without Sister Rose Ann Fleming. She arrived on campus in 1982 and I arrived two years later. I came as a history professor and went on to become President. She came as an academic adviser and went on to become a legend.

She took on a task back in 1985 that, on the surface, appears to be fun and filled with perks. She worked with the most high profile student-athletes on campus to help build a basketball program that would catapult a small, Jesuit university, known for rigorous academics, into the national NCAA Division One spotlight.

Well, we're there. And the five-foot-four, barely 100-pound, no-nonsense powerhouse that we all call Sister is a big reason why.

We're known for bragging that we've graduated every senior men's basketball player since 1986 and that we're consistently one of the top fifteen schools in the nation when it comes to overall student-athlete graduation success rate. Between 2004 and 2014 we've made it to the NCAA basketball Elite Eight twice, made five total Sweet 16 appearances and we're one of only thirteen schools to make at least eight NCAA basketball tournaments in the last nine years.

Sister has been at the forefront of paving the way to achieve those bragging rights, which now help define Xavier. Yes, there was some fun along the way, like when she was named the team's Most Valuable Player in 1991 and inducted into Xavier's Athletic Hall of Fame in 2000.

Perks? It all depends on your definition. Great seats for all home and away games? Definitely a perk. Dinner of lukewarm pizza straight out of the box, sitting on a bus at 11 p.m. after an away game and a loss? Not so much. But Sister has been there for it all—the wins, the losses, the benchings, the personal struggles, the gentle (and not so gentle) nudging to stay on track academically to remain eligible athletically.

Three decades of defining, creating, maintaining and continually refining athletic academic advising, with a personal focus on men's basketball, has been a monumental challenge and labor of love for Sister Rose Ann. The phenomenal success of her efforts has brought national recognition for both her and Xavier. She has been profiled in the *New York Times, Washington Post,* ABC News, NBC News and FoxSports, among many others.

Sister has mastered the art of juggling her academic and legal careers with her vocation as a Sister of Notre Dame de Namur. But her complete dedication and focused attention to the Xavier men's basketball program has allowed our program and our

University as a whole to excel and thrive in ways that were unimaginable before she arrived on campus.

In 2015 we'll mark thirty years since Sister founded Student-Athlete Academic Support Services. During the 2014–2015 basketball season, we'll honor her and celebrate the success she has achieved by hanging a jersey with her name from the rafters of the Cintas Center along with the other heroes of Xavier basketball…West, Hill, Larkin, Hoff. Future generations will see "Fleming" and know that you don't have to be six-foot-six and have an even larger wingspan to make a difference on a basketball team.

As Sister says, "They need to understand that you really love them. If they know they're loved, they'll do almost anything to achieve." Amen to that.

—Michael J. Graham, S.J.
President, Xavier University

Prologue

Despite bitter wind and a mean, gritty snow, the 10,250-seat Cintas Center at Xavier University is packed, and the crowd is warming up. In the stands, students wave a gigantic cardboard likeness of Pope Francis. It's an exuberant tribute to the world's best-known Jesuit at a university that comfortably embraces Ignatian values, even at a basketball game.

Nikes screech against hardwood, the sound made by big feet whose owners may someday sign their names on similarly expensive and noisy shoes. The lights are dazzling. Music throbs through a new sound system, and action photos beam from an enormous center-hung scoreboard, bounty from a recent multimillion-dollar electronic tune-up. A lighted ribbon board snakes around the inside perimeter with player stats, NCAA game scores and sponsor messages.

It's human nature to keep score, especially in athletics. Who won, who lost, who signed an NBA contract for the most money. The numbers are sliced and diced and charted and graphed and turned inside out. They cling like sea lamprey to an athlete or a coach. It's not enough to know that sophomore guard Semaj Christon scores 18 points against Georgetown that night. Meticulous records will capture his total performance—9-of-12 shooting, four rebounds and one assist.

A coach's record not only includes his percentage of wins, but his wins in tournament games, close games, blowout games and overtime games. Musketeer head coach Chris Mack, sharp-featured and intense, scribbles on his whiteboard during a time-out. Some bad numbers. The Georgetown University Hoyas are ahead by 17.

With two minutes left, I abandon my choice seat just behind the bench, and by the time the Musketeers roar from behind to win, 80–67, I am waiting at the door of their locker room. They come bounding toward me, young faces shining with sweat and the win, pounding me gently on the back, throwing vascular tattooed arms around my shoulders.

They knew I would be there. I generally am, at home and on the road, to celebrate or to console. This $46-million arena was built and the seats filled by young men playing ball for this Jesuit Catholic institution on the east side of Cincinnati. They draw attention to our school and TV money to the university coffers.

I am here to thank them for their hard work. I know how hard they work because I have been keeping another detailed set of team stats—their GPAs, their class attendance, their papers due, their test scores, their academic credit hours. I have been their tutor.

Their wake-up call. Their confidant. Their nag. Their life coach. For thirty years, I have been Xavier University's academic coordinator for its athletes, and during that time, 100 percent of the young men who have played basketball for Xavier University as seniors left with a diploma. All of them. Every one. No matter where they started, they ended up with a documented, charted and official education from an excellent school. We recruit them, and they sign up to work for us. I believe it's fair and right that they get a real education in the bargain.

Ready to leave the game, two minutes before the buzzer.

For twenty of those thirty years, I've worked with players in all of Xavier's eighteen sports, but most of my time has been spent with basketball players. The reason is simple—they were the ones who needed me most. Some of them came to our campus with what is delicately described as educational deficiencies, which meant they had a lot of catching up to do. Others had attitude: "Basketball is why I'm here. Not books."

Sometimes I have been as welcome as a case of athlete's foot.

When they sign on, they are getting a chance a lot of other students never have: leaving college with a degree and no debt. So I have pushed and prodded, cajoled and threatened, keenly aware that besides their studies, they are working at an exhausting job for young men barely out of high school. They are in a gym twenty or more hours a week, with one day a week travel on school nights. They are watched, analyzed and criticized by everyone from NBA recruiters to the casual couch potato fans.

Some have been waved through indifferent public and parochial schools, which have celebrated their athletic gifts and ignored their educational shortfalls. Sometimes spoiled, sometimes neglected, they can be willful, wary and volatile. They are not, not, not stupid. Anybody who is smart enough to memorize hundreds of complicated basketball plays can surely pass a test in biology or write a philosophy paper. I just have to figure out how to help them find the way. And convince them that the numbers and letters they earn with their heads are just as important—and will follow them just as ruthlessly through life—as their free throw percentage or their fast break points.

That said, here are my personal numbers: I am five feet, four inches tall. I'm usually identified by my age—82. And, inevitably, by my vocation. I am a nun.

Out of HABIT

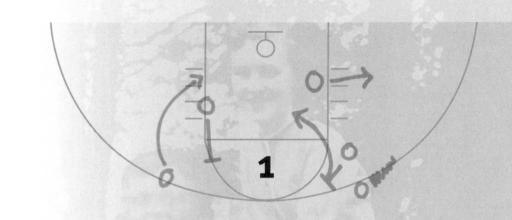

1

A Minor Rebellion

Mother, Tom, and I before our terrible loss.

$\mathcal{P}$art of the cachet that has propelled me to the front pages of sports sections and onto network television is the contrast, the novelty of a very small, very white woman surrounded by young men of color who are a foot and a half taller and six decades younger. Occasionally, a report will note that during a privileged life, I earned a law degree, two master's degrees and a Ph.D simply to help an inner city hoops star pursue an undergraduate degree. It's icing on the media cake that I am a member of a religious order who gave up a job as president of a prestigious university to work in a classroom.

The truth is that I have far more in common with these young athletes than anyone would guess. In fact, our work together seems perfectly logical to me, and I believe every step along the way—from Cincinnati to the cloister to Washington, D.C., and back— led directly to these young men in this specific institution and taught me something they could use. And I have given up nothing.

My very first steps in life were in tandem with my twin brother, Tom. Was I the first one on my feet when we were toddlers? I'd like to think so. I am very competitive, and I do not believe winning is an acquired taste. Tom's wife, Theresa, has a colorized photo of us at about age 4. We were blond and scrubbed. I was in a pale orchid smocked pinafore with a matching bow in my hair, Tom in short pants. In those days before permanent press and automatic washing machines and dryers, our clothes nonetheless were immaculate and crisp, our white shoes polished.

We look like children who were treasured, and I believe we were. My parents lost our older brother to what was called crib death ten days after they brought him home from the hospital. They prayed for another child, and they got me and, a minute later, my brother. The power of prayer was very potent in our family.

In fact, Mother used it once to make an end run around my father. Our pretty Irish mother was energetic and warm. Dad, more sober and traditional, was a CPA who worked long hours. He adored our mother and would have been content if she had spent all her considerable energy on himself and us. As we left the toddler stage, she wanted to take a more active role in our parish church, but Dad objected. Right about that time, Tom fell out of a tree and was knocked unconscious for a few minutes. Mom and Dad rushed him to the hospital, where they were assured he had suffered no real harm.

On the trip home, Mom announced to my father that she had promised God if he spared Tom she would join the Catholic Sodality service group, which she did immediately and enthusiastically.

Despite Dad's reservations, she was always waiting at the door for us when we got home from school. When I was in the second grade, one of my teachers called my mother to tattle. I was wasteful, she said, squandering paper towels in the bathroom. In our one-paper-towel-to-a-customer world, this was a major extravagance. I denied it, and held up my small hands to my mother as mute testimony. Really, would any reasonable person think it took a lot of the school's paper to get them dry? Mom didn't hesitate. She took my side. "If you say you didn't, you didn't."

Having somebody listen to you and believe what you tell them is deeply significant to a youngster. I would have many occasions to remember this simple lesson and put it to use on other people's children.

The paper towel wastrel in the second grade at The Summit.

Mom read somewhere that twins should be pried apart as they grew older, so they'd develop as individuals. From kindergarten through high school, I attended The Summit Country Day School, a Catholic private school for girls in Cincinnati. Tom was allowed to attend the separate elementary school there for boys but later was sent downtown to the Jesuit equivalent for older boys, St. Xavier.

But when we were little, we did most things together, including the despised Saturday morning dance classes at the Cincinnati Art Museum.

Afterward, we'd go to the Frisch's Mainliner for milkshakes and a Big Boy. A reward, I guess. Bribery would certainly not be something my father would approve. Even better, when we were a little older, Mom treated us to horseback riding lessons in the afternoon at a stable off Red Bank Road, fairly near our house. Tom and I galloped around the ring while our mother watched, biting her lip, clutching her Rosary beads and praying for our safety. I loved everything about it—the wind in my face, the horses, my jodhpurs.

I knew I would never fall off.

For a while, life seemed nearly perfect. Then Mom began having back aches, and we knew she was very sick. One memory haunts me still. I was standing by her bed and she said tiredly, "Oh, Rose Ann, I don't think I can take you to your horseback riding lesson this week."

"Oh, that's okay. Aunt Mary will take us." I knew how wrong that was as soon as it was out of my mouth. She was irreplaceable.

Mother died when I was 11. It was cancer. Tom and I missed her dreadfully. Tom still tears up when he says, "I just missed talking to her so much." My anguish detoured toward anger. After Mother died, I didn't like nuns and I didn't like sitting in class. I burned up a lot of energy on the hockey field, running, running, running, but I still had too much spirit left for Sister Anna Regis.

Behind her back, we called her Sister Anna Rages, and a large share of her rage was lavished on me. Looking back, I can see that I was pretty much out of control. I was routinely thrown out of the library for talking. I questioned authority. Is that the way it has to be done? And, of course, I was known to be profligate with paper towels. I ruined the class production of *Song of Bernadette* by scattering sticks and leaves all over the stage instead of sweeping them neatly into a pile. I didn't bother to tell a livid and rampaging Sister Anna Regis that I had never seen anybody use a broom and thought for once I was doing exactly as she'd asked.

I was not rebellious, just uninformed, another lesson I would tuck away for later use. But at the time, I just put on my coat and walked home.

Later on, I cemented my reputation as a trouble-maker by leading three of my classmates up to the roof of The Summit's thrillingly mysterious five-story main building. Designed by the world famous architect Edwin Forrest Durang in the Romanesque style beloved by the church and particularly by the Sisters of Notre Dame de Namur, who hired him to work on their Trinity College in Washington, D.C., it was built in 1890. We cared little for its history, but we loved the view. The Ohio River snaked to the east, and we could see behind the gates of some of the nearby Grandin Road estates. Best of all, it was strictly forbidden, off-limits, which was even more exciting than the panoramic vista. We left a door open, and I was identified as the ring leader in an impressively short time.

I was too young for prison. The principal recommended boarding school.

More than fifty years later, I thought of The Summit and that frightful broom when I met Tyrone Hill. Tall and aggressive, he could dominate a basketball court, even as a freshman at Xavier. He also had a chip on his shoulder the size of a Volkswagen and a glower that could blister paint. Of course, I liked him right away. He was about to flunk a class because he couldn't—or wouldn't—write a paper that was due. I steered him over to the library. He cursed under his breath. A single hissing expletive, the same word, over and over, almost in time with our footsteps. Lacking a dignified response, I just kept walking briskly, hoping he would follow. He did.

He was smart and curious, and at first he just watched, paying close attention to students as they went about their research, pulling books off the shelves, copying documents, making notes, asking for and getting help from the librarians. And I watched him. It was like a cartoon light bulb switching on over my head. This young man doesn't know how to use a library. He hasn't a clue that everything he needs to finish his paper is here, available to him. There is no worse feeling than knowing there is an "in" crowd and you're not in it. Embarrassed that he didn't have this basic skill, he was as likely to confess his ignorance to his professor as I would have been to tell Sister Anna Regis. I admired the fact that he didn't just put on his coat and go home.

Tyrone and I had lots more work to do together. He did not miraculously turn into a scholar, but I had the keys now and would use them shamelessly to challenge him during his years at the university. Proud. Observant. Able to connect the dots. He turned out to be the first really great athlete I worked with, and he played in the National Basketball Association (NBA) for several years before becoming a coach. My allies when we were locked together in the great paper chase for a diploma were, of course, the resources at the university, his tutors and professors and even administration. But I also was in league with his family.

During my years at Xavier, I would appreciate many times the profound influence of family. Tyrone's friend and teammate Byron Larkin is a terrific example. Another talented player and a good guy, he was one of five kids raised in Silverton, Ohio, by Robert and Shirley Larkin. Their house was a gathering place for kids and once a persnickety neighbor complained about bare spots on the Larkin lawn. Robert told the man he'd rather raise children than grass. Byron's younger brother Barry, a Hall of Fame shortstop for the Cincinnati Reds, was benched in high school by his parents when his Latin grade wasn't up to snuff. They soon reversed their decision. Shirley says, "It just didn't work. He was a much better student when he was playing sports. Sometimes I think that's what parents don't do—notice what works for this child. They're not all the same."

My own family overruled the recommendation to banish me to boarding school and shrouded me in attention. Dad's sister and his mother came to live with us, and I was allowed to continue wearing my brown and peach Summit uniform and stay in our house on a beautiful tree-lined street in Mt. Lookout on Cincinnati's east side. Both Tom and I continued to compete in sports, compete being the operative word. Team sports offered me a tremendous sense of belonging. I played field hockey, softball, volleyball and basketball, but as I grew older, there was another team I wanted to join. It may have started with a teacher named Sister Teresa Mary McCarthy. One day she pulled me aside and said, "I think you are a very interesting person."

"Why?" I wondered.

She laughed and said, "Well for one thing, every time I see you in the hall you are standing against the wall while Sister Anna Regis shouts at you."

She had singled me out. Interesting, she called me. That was a whole lot better than what I had been hearing. I knew she liked me, had noticed me. She wasn't Mother, but I thought maybe I could count on her to listen. Maybe I had somebody in the building who was on my side. My grades began to improve, and school no longer seemed so dismal. My best friend, Pat O'Keefe, was smart and got good grades, so rivalry might also have played a role. I tucked away two more lessons for my future Xavier University students: simply knowing a teacher likes you can be a life preserver to a drowning student. And a competitive temperament can be channeled beyond a basketball court.

My teachers at The Summit were Sisters of Notre Dame de Namur. Founded in Belgium during the era of Robespierre, the teaching order's mission was to help "the poorest of the poor" through education. From the inception of the order, they had a mission of working with people of means to help the poor. Our

Eighth grade rebellion quelled.

teachers swept through the polished wood corridors of The Summit in imposing long black habits with bright white collars and wimples, and their stories were equally dramatic. I was fascinated by the order's adventures in China, Africa, Japan, Peru and the Brazilian Amazon, as well as Europe.

The theme was consistent: education is the key to survival—a notion that surely is part of my DNA. The order's first American foundation was established in Cincinnati. So maybe I was hearing the message from the most persuasive, committed and talented of our order.

> Dad thought if I kept my date with the Sisters of Notre Dame de Namur, I would never get out again for the rest of my life.

We had a three-day retreat during my sophomore year in high school. We were told to bring knitting needles to make argyle socks while we listened to lectures and meditated. I had exactly as much experience with knitting needles as I did with a broom, but I did think and pray and listen. My motherless heart was touched. God loves me, I thought. I was drawn to that, to the concept of God. He loves you. He needs nothing but he loves you. There was no bolt of lightning, no huge revelations. I left the retreat without ever finishing a single diamond on a sock but with my sights set on joining the order and devoting my life to Him.

My father had other ideas.

My grades at The Summit continued to improve. Dad taught Tom and me how to play golf at Kenwood Country Club. Tom had to caddy for him, but the girl child got to ride in a cart. I was happier and made friends with my classmates, who elected me president during my final year. On Friday nights, Dad and I often went out to dinner and a movie downtown. Tom usually was, as he puts it, "out with the boys." Nobody had to pry us apart now. We were definitely individuals.

Dinner alone with Dad was a good chance to talk, and when I was a senior in high school, I ruined a perfectly nice meal at the male-members-only Cincinnati Club by telling him I wanted to join the religious order after graduation from The Summit.

Dad carefully put down his knife and fork and just looked at me. The next day, he went to my high school and met with the principal, who was a Sister of Notre Dame. I don't know exactly what was said, but Dad told me he had promised my mother that Tom and I would go to college and promised Sister he would pay for it. After college, I would go to Europe with Aunt Mary, he said. Then I could decide what to do. Tom says Dad was very proud of me and simply wanted to contribute. "He wanted to finance

Aunt Mary and I in Ireland, welcomed by our Irish cousins during Dad's Last Chance to Change Your Mind European Tour.

Rose Ann's college education. It was his way of helping."

I think he wanted me to change my mind.

For the next four years, I studied at the College of Mount St. Joseph, a Catholic liberal arts college run by the Sisters of Charity on the outskirts of Cincinnati. I boarded there, but Dad or Tom drove forty-five minutes every Friday night to pick me up and take me home.

"As soon as she got home, she opened a book," Tom says. "She really loved to study. She spent most of the weekend in her room with her books." I remember having a lot more fun than that. During my last three years at Mount St. Joe, I was elected class president and discovered a knack for fund raising and organization, mostly setting up a hot dog concession to raise money for dances. I went to those dances and flirted with boys from Xavier University. I had a social drink or two, but never developed a taste for alcohol. I was not a drudge, but I always knew where I was headed.

After graduation from the College of Mount St. Joseph, Aunt Mary and I left on the grand trip to Europe my father had promised and planned. It had to be something special, because Dad thought if I kept my date with the Sisters of Notre Dame de Namur, I would never get out again for the rest of my life. He set up a gondola ride in Venice and an audience with Pope Pius XII at the papal summer home, Castel Gandolfo near Rome.

Aunt Mary had more worldly interests, including shopping and an evening at the Folies Bergere in Paris. A good Catholic girl, I enjoyed the music but closed my eyes at the racy stuff. Of course, my idea of a good time was to trek to the Notre Dame de Namur motherhouse in Belgium. I knelt, said a prayer in the chapel and noticed that Rue de la Billiart looked a lot like Sixth Street in downtown Cincinnati.

We visited Lourdes and loaded up with bottles of holy water, available now on Amazon for $3.95, but which were priceless to Aunt Mary in that summer of 1954. We visited our Irish cousins, kissed the Blarney Stone then came home with our smuggled cache of holy water, back to the United States and to my destiny.

I entered the Sisters of Notre Dame convent on Sept. 8, 1954. I was 22 years old.

Once again, Dad was outflanked by prayer and a promise.

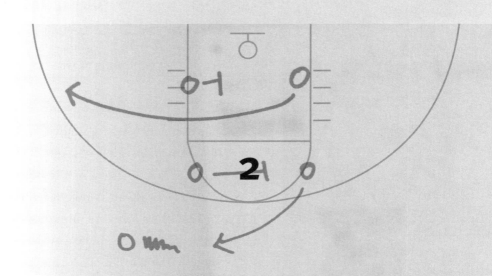

Life as
Sister Thomas Mary

President of my class at Mount St. Joseph
College, where I studied the classics and
hot dog vending.

Sometimes people know you well enough to ask—don't you miss having children and a husband? Was it hard to surrender yourself to the will of the convent, of the church, of other nuns? Or even, what I suspect they really want to know, did you have to shave your head? When I think back to those high school retreats when I did not knit socks but instead came to God, when I remember the feeling of security, of love, of purpose, of happiness, I want to ask instead, why would I choose anything else?

Once you enter religious life, you are given to understand that what you are told to do is the will of God. The will of God mostly was passed along to us through the postulant mistress, and I was astonished that His will involved so much furniture polish and cornbread. Hard work—polishing and cleaning—was not something I minded. The cornbread was another matter and led to many penitent hours on my knees in the communal dining room.

On the day I officially entered, Aunt Mary, Dad and Tom took me to the Notre Dame de Namur convent in Reading, a suburb just north of Cincinnati. They stayed for a beautiful benediction drifting on the aroma of incense. As soon as they left, I and the twelve other postulants, which is what you are called when you are a candidate to join the order, handed over the few possessions we'd brought with us and exchanged the clothes we'd worn for identical black blouses, skirts and sweaters. The clothes weren't bad, even the big black net cap that hung on the back of my head, but the shoes were awful. Also black, they were stiff and laced. I called them "trotters." Later I learned that my students made fun of our "ground grippers." It was the double whammy: ugly and uncomfortable.

Our narrow beds were in a row with curtain partitions, leaving just enough room for a small dresser and a straight-backed wood chair. I didn't need anything more, and I mean that sincerely. The spartan furnishings made sense. The vow of poverty wasn't punishment. Life was simplified, which would leave us more time to think about important matters and to work, meditate and pray. Although unimpeded by material concerns, almost immediately, my life became fuller and busier than I had expected.

I arrived on Saturday. The next day, I was told that a teacher at nearby Mt. Notre Dame Academy had suffered a heart attack and that I was to take over her classes Monday. Also, two of the postulants hadn't finished high school, so I was assigned to tutor them. Wake-up call was at 4:55 in the morning, giving us a half hour to get dressed and ready for the day and five minutes to walk to the chapel. Luckily, I have never needed much sleep and I craved activity. Even today, my chosen routine is getting up at 4 a.m. to meditate and pray, then I run four or five miles or work out on an elliptical machine and free weights in my little room in the Manor House, an apartment complex where many athletes have lived. This has been handy when I needed to pound on doors to rouse somebody for class.

Back then, I headed off to Mt. Notre Dame Academy to pick up the history of Europe where the stricken Sister Helene had left off. The girls knew I was a rookie, but they never took advantage. One young girl, in particular, told me something I would remember many years later when a dejected basketball player named Lenny Brown gave up on Xavier University. "The teacher doesn't like me," he said. Just that simple. And that complicated.

As if it was yesterday, I can see Jane Gilligan Albers leaning across my scarred teacher's desk in her blue and white uniform, wide eyes earnest. "I get good grades because I like you." Students learn better when they know the teacher likes them.

Returning to my alma mater as Sister Thomas Mary to teach Latin.

When I started teaching, I was focused on covering the material, but what Jane said was something I had totally missed. The relationship.

So, long before he was born, Jane handed me the key to a complicated and troubled boy who came to play basketball at Xavier in the late 1990s. Lenny Brown always was happiest when he was playing basketball, and it was a constant battle to get him to aim a little of that enthusiasm toward his studies. He would show up in class at Xavier with his hoodie up and drawn so only his eyes were visible. Inside his hoodie were headphones. He was incommunicado.

Finally, he just left. Packed up his stuff and got on a bus. The head coach, Skip Prosser at the time, missed him at practice and sent his assistant, Jeff Battle, to track Lenny down. One of the players said Lenny was going home to Delaware. Jeff and Jay Ross, a trainer everybody called The Healer, raced up Interstate 71 to what they were hoping was Lenny's first stop—Columbus. They arrived just in time. He was finishing up a video game as his connecting bus pulled into the station.

The two of them collared Lenny and persuaded him to go back to campus with them. Jeff was very popular and respected by all the players, and I'm sure he made a good case for giving Xavier another go. Jay Ross was called The Healer and not just because of his position as trainer. I think he healed our young men in other ways. He was a strong role model and very, very sympathetic and intuitive. It would have been hard for Lenny not to listen to these two excellent men.

Lenny called me that night, and I promised I would try to help him if he came to see me the next day. When I came out of church, he was waiting for me, sitting on the steps. He was failing biology.

"Lenny, are you sure?"

"She told me so. And she doesn't like me."

He was really down in the dumps and talked about an incident in class in which the teacher had congratulated another athlete, a swimmer, on a medal he'd won. "She never said anything to me," he said, which sounds childish and petulant until you remember that basketball was the only thing Lenny thought he had going for him. "When I come back from road trips, she never talks about the game. She just tells me what I missed and wants to know when I can make it up."

"That's hard to take, isn't it?" I said, and at that moment I think I realized how hard it really was for him, how much basketball meant to him. Once the cheering stopped, he felt worthless. If anybody needed an education, a backup plan, this young man did. We talked for a long time, and I told him we might have a chance if his teacher would agree to give him an incomplete instead of an F and more time to make up the work. He'd missed some classes and two experiments while he was on the road with the team, so he had a legitimate case.

"You'll have to ask her," I said. "I'll go with you."

He did, and she agreed. I called the chair of the biology department, Dr. Charles Grossman, a wonderful man, and explained the situation—and the at-risk student—as best I could. The biology chair said, "If Lenny makes a contract with me, I will let him take the test."

The contract was simple and non-negotiable. Lenny had to promise to do all the reading assignments. The chair arranged to duplicate the experiments and lab work Lenny had missed while traveling with the team. Lenny had to promise to be there. On time, paying attention, taking notes. It wouldn't hurt, I told him, if he'd loosen his hood every once and a while. Smile now and then.

We got him a tutor, and he kept every promise he'd made. He passed and kept his eligibility. He earned plenty of accolades for his play over the course of his career at Xavier, including two times on the Atlantic-10 First Team, once on the A-10 second Team and once on the A-10 All-Rookie Team. In addition, he made the final John R. Wooden Award All-America nominee list and earned a spot on the 1999 All-National Invitation Tournament team.

Best of all, from my point of view, he earned a degree from Xavier University in 1999. Skip used to call Lenny a "courageous player," aggressive, exciting to watch. But asking a favor of somebody he thought didn't like him, didn't respect his worth, was the bravest thing I ever saw him do.

Lenny taught me an important lesson or maybe just reminded me of one I had learned as a rebellious child, drowning in anger until Sister Teresa Mary McCarthy tossed me a life preserver. Jane Gilligan Albers gave me another nudge when I was a young teacher at Mt. Notre Dame. "Students learn better when they know you like them." Lenny taught me later that the flip side also is very true. If young people don't think you like them, if you don't respect the abilities they have, they will shut you out. They care.

A counselor across the hall from my classroom at Mt. Notre Dame showed me the corollary to Jane and Teresa Mary's lessons. Nearly sixty years later, I can still hear the cheerful voice of Sister Mary Constance, smiling and greeting students as if they were exactly the person she'd been hoping to see that day. She made them feel important, sounding as if it was a pleasure to serve them. Most of the students came directly from the principal's office, so I imagine they needed that reassurance as they were usually fresh from a scolding. That's good, I thought. I want to be like that. I tried to sound like her. I still do.

At the convent, I was locked in a battle of wills with Sister Juliana. To this day, I don't understand why refusing to load up my plate with a big square of rough, dry cornbread got me in so much trouble. Refusal to eat what was put before me was seen as a sign of defiance, I guess, or maybe word had reached Sister Juliana that I had never been properly disciplined for my wasteful nature. She made me kneel at the table in penitence. I nibbled on a little square. Not enough. More kneeling. Like clothes, food has never been very important to me. I don't eat red meat and mostly choose salads or vegetables with maybe a little fish or chicken when I get the chance. But at the convent, you ate what was put on the table. I'm sure she thought it was for my own good. But I didn't think she liked me.

Despite encounters with the protector of paper towels and the keeper of cornbread, my experiences with my sisters has been one of almost universal generosity and kindness. While I was at the convent I learned a lot about the French woman who founded our order and who set the tone for our work today. Paralyzed as a young girl, Marie Rose Julie Billiart nonetheless drew people to her. She was said to be cheerful and full of joy, magnetic. Her characteristic phrase was: "How good is the good God! He is, He's around and He's good." All this love and faith was despite being butchered by doctors who tried repeated bloodletting to cure her infirmity.

She continued to speak openly to a growing number of followers, ignoring the danger of a message that was heresy to French Jansenists, who favored what my friend Sister Mary Ann Barnhorn calls a "gotcha God," ready to pounce and send you to hell if you didn't toe the line.

Sister Mary Ann, who's director of development for our order and one of our most eloquent storytellers, recounts the history of the founding of the Sisters of Notre Dame de Namur in 1803, when St. Julie Billiart was still paralyzed and spoke with difficulty. Countess Marie-Louise-Francoise Blin de Bourdon came to her for

16

Still at Summit, but now as Sister Rose Ann, animal-loving administrator with Antigone, the "house dog."

spiritual direction and became a strategic ally. St. Julie had a warm spirituality. The countess had money. Together they founded an order to rescue poor girls from the street through education.

Shortly afterward, St. Julie regained the use of her legs and her voice and the miracle propelled her long miles on foot throughout France and Belgium. The two women would trudge off to the nearest city and ring a bell, summoning street girls to class. They financed free schools for the poor with tuition and fees from day schools and academies they operated for the daughters of middle class and wealthy families. St. Julie died in April of 1816 and was canonized in 1969. Her message of education is still fresh, and I've always been proud of the resourceful ways my sisters continue St. Julie Billiart's work throughout the world.

Today the Sisters of Notre Dame de Namur serve in seventeen countries on five continents, but their first mission abroad was to Cincinnati at the request of Archbishop John Purcell. Eight women from our order sailed across the Atlantic, landing in New York, going by rail to Pittsburgh and finally down the Ohio, arriving in Cincinnati Oct. 13, 1840. The then-Bishop Purcell set them up in the

Spencer mansion on Sixth Street, cater-corner to St. Xavier Church, downtown, and from there they offered a classical European education to girls who had been taught the three R's at best.

The sisters gave lessons in geography, history and the fine arts, along with science taught with equipment they'd hauled over on the ship. Daughters of the wealthy and of the poor got the identical opportunity for learning, just as it had been done in St. Julie's day—with tuition and fees from the wealthy financing education in the slums. This school and convent was the model for new parish schools and academies in other areas of Ohio and eventually Illinois, Massachusetts, Maryland and the entire East Coast. These women swept right into the eye of the storm, into cities crumbling under the masses of people streaming into them from farms, looking for work during the industrial revolution.

All that's left of the trailblazing sisters' original Cincinnati home are the marble columned Spencer mansion doors, which are in the Cincinnati Art Museum. Procter & Gamble's headquarters sprawl on the site of the home. Samples of exquisite lace made by the nuns and their students and an old contraption depicting planets revolving around the sun are preserved in the museum at our Province Center in Reading, where the Mount Notre Dame campus also includes the Health Center, St. Julie Chapel, St. Julie Community, Spirituality Center, Archives and Province Offices.

*T*he spirit of St. Julie and her symbiotic vision still watches over us, no matter where we are. At a meeting about our mission in Africa, I watched with interest as Sister Mary Ann's assistant, Karen Hadden, plunked a big jar of dirty water on the table. She then dumped the contents of a little packet into it, demonstrating how the water could then be purified to drink. Our order has forged an alliance with Procter & Gamble to bring clean drinking water to rural Africa by distributing these little packets of PUR, along with a demonstration like the one I saw. Each packet, about the size of a fast-food packet of sweetener, can purify two and a half gallons of river or well water.

It's St. Julie Billiart's specialty updated: helping the poor through education with support from the prosperous.

Becoming a vowed member of my order happens gradually, and history is only part of the process. Like Dad, they gave us plenty of time and information in case we wanted to change our minds. After six months as a postulant, I started my novitiate. Then after I had been living at the convent for six months, I began what is known as the canonical year and donned the habit. When Dad came to visit, he didn't recognize me. He really didn't know who I was. On top of that, I had a new name symbolizing my new life. A lot of sisters chose their mother's and father's names, if appropriate. You didn't hear of many Sister Elmer Elaines or Barbara Dentons, but luckily, my parents' names worked just fine. Mary and Thomas. Somebody had already chosen Mary Thomas, so I just switched them around, giving Dad top billing. I thought he'd be pleased.

"That is not what we named you," he said stiffly.

Dad was a hard sell.

During the canonical year, our instruction in the gospels, the new and old testament and the history of our order intensified. I didn't see my family at all, but Tom, my dear sentimental brother, wrote every week from Stuttgart, Germany, where he was a commissioned Army officer. My whole family was there when I made my final vows. I continued to teach at Mt. Notre Dame, adding English and Latin to my repertoire.

> **My dear, faithful, skeptical father continued to keep his promise to my mother that I would go to college, but he probably never guessed that I would go to so many of them.**

One evening in September of 1960, when I knelt to pray in my accustomed spot in the convent chapel, I found a thin, white envelope. It was what we called a mission, and inside was a terse directive. I was to teach Latin at my alma mater, The Summit Country Day School. Starting immediately. I was disappointed to learn that Sister Teresa Mary had recently left the school for another post, so she wouldn't be there to see if I had turned out to be as interesting as she predicted.

Summit had a residence for teachers on the fourth floor of the main building. The principal, Sister Marie Emilie Walsh, had a TV in her office tuned to *Good Morning America*, and I was happy to escape my breakfast cornbread—that stuff was everywhere— and join her. She encouraged us, especially the high school teachers, to watch GMA's Joan Lunden and David Hartman for a half hour every morning before class. She wanted us to know what was happening in the outside world, a somewhat progressive notion.

This was before Vatican II, when the rules for nuns were very strict, pretty much what they'd been for a century. When Tom married Theresa, in 1961, I wasn't permitted to go to the ceremony at Theresa's church in Norwood, even though it was Catholic. Change was in the wind, but not just yet. Anyway, there were no rules that said the wedding couldn't come to me.

Right after the official Mass at St. Matthew's Church, Tom and Theresa tucked her gorgeous satin dress into their car and drove to the chapel at The Summit, where they repeated their walk down the aisle. Tom cried every step of the way. Over their next several years of married life, they were kind enough to present Dad with five grandchildren, which took some of the heat off me. Dad was also pleased when I eventually reclaimed the name he and my mother had given me.

My dear, faithful, skeptical father continued to keep his promise to my mother that I would go to college, but he probably never guessed that I would go to so many of them. He wrote checks and chauffeured me—to Detroit, where I earned a master's in Victorian and 19th Century English. I drove myself to Xavier for my master's in education, but Dad was back behind the wheel when I was working on a Ph.D from Miami University in educational administration.

Besides stacking new letters into my resume, I was continually enriched by people I met outside the sphere of my church. There are so many openhearted and generous people in this world. The religious don't have a corner on goodness, and all knowledge doesn't come from books. I loved arguing politics and discussing movies and, well, just picking up shards of wisdom wherever I found them.

Sometimes I wonder if what people call intellectual curiosity is simply a lifelong habit of learning. I honestly had no intention of piling up degrees, but all these schools had something I needed to know. At least I thought so.

The title of my doctoral dissertation was typically catchy: "The Relationship Between Administrative Behavior of the Principal and the Quality of Multi-Dimensional Organizational Output of Schools as Assessed By Teachers and Administrators of Catholic Elementary and Secondary Schools." All right, I know that name would cure a raging case of insomnia. But, in fact, all it says is to keep the troops happy.

X

After I'd been at The Summit about three years, Sister Marie Emilie asked me to take over the liaison job with alumni and parents. I helped plan fund-raisers, which were more complicated than the hot dog stand at Mount St. Joseph, but this time I had help from an eclectic and shrewd board of trustees. In 1967, I was promoted to superintendent of the school with an admonition from the Order saying, in effect, "Times are tough. Good luck, but don't ask for any more personnel or money."

> **How would I keep the troops happy and the wolf from the door at the same time?**

My heart dropped. I was looking at a daunting ledger. Nuns worked for $5,000 a year. Lay personnel cost considerably more. The operations budget was already stained with red ink. How would I keep the troops happy and the wolf from the door at the same time?

Jim Brockhoff, who later was Xavier University's head tennis coach and a fund-raising dynamo, was then headmaster at The Summit. A Cincinnati boy and a standout athlete at Purcell High School and Xavier, Jim seemed to know everybody in town and was terrifically helpful. I also turned to the alumni and the now-familiar board members for help. Many of them were businessmen with secular ideas they translated into smart maneuvers for my religious academic world.

One of my favorites on the board was John "Bud" Koons III, president of Burger Brewing Co., whose mantra was simply: "Fill the factory. Get more bodies in the seats." For the next eight years, we did just that, increasing enrollment by 66 percent and erasing the operating deficit.

We also expanded the "factory," establishing a four-year boys college prep high school and a new primary school. Louis G. Freeman Jr., who pioneered an employee stock purchase plan at his company, was on the board when we increased faculty salaries by 55 percent. I always fought to pay our faculty and staff as much as we could possibly afford. Of course, I wanted them to be happy. That would be more pleasant for me, but I also believe getting the best people and keeping them is good business. Turnover is expensive. And quality begets quality.

We weren't really running a factory. We weren't manufacturing widgets. We were doing something more crucial than bottling beer. We were nurturing and teaching children, and we should hold ourselves to the highest standard and do our best to attract the most capable people.

We also bolstered our already successful Montessori program. When Mario Montessori, son of the founder of this method, came to inspect our program, he told us about two schools in the east he thought might interest us.

Typically, The Summit's responsive board pulled through with airline tickets for a couple of us to go ahead to make arrangements to visit the Dalton School on Manhatten's Upper East Side and the Whitby School in Greenwich, Connecticut. Then Jim Brockhoff's friend Harry Hocks, who owned a Buick dealership, lent us a fleet of cars for staff to follow. We exchanged ideas with faculty at both schools, other educators who believed passionately in the development of the whole child, who believed schools should devote themselves to the total enrichment of mind, body and spirit.

It was a recipe for success that helped in my work with athletes I would meet years later at Xavier University, and it sounded a lot like what I would hear from the Jesuits there. But I had miles to go first.

Another little white envelope arrived.

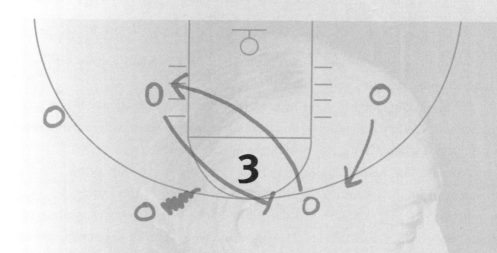

3

High Finance and a Papal Visit

Installed as president of Trinity College in its historic Notre Dame Chapel.

*I*n many ways, Trinity College was like The Summit, except the pool of red ink was deeper and I was a lot farther from home.

This assignment had given me pause. After I read the words in my mission envelope summoning me to interview for the position of president of a college in Washington, D.C., I went to The Summit's chapel. Trinity College founder Sister Julia Moriarty was buried there. I lay flat on her tomb and prayed. Before my eyes was a stone etched with the words: "Not to us, oh Lord, not to us but to your name give glory." Okay. I was getting the message. Maybe all those degrees were pointing somewhere. Maybe the direction was out of town, out of my comfort zone.

The trustees didn't want to send the faculty and other Trinity personnel into a tailspin, so we met in secret at an airport in Washington. Trinity's Charter specified that someone from the founding order—Sisters of Notre Dame de Namur—had to preside over the College, and I supposed I was one of the few in our order who had a Ph.D in educational administration. They asked a lot of questions about erasing The Summit's $350,000 operating deficit and about increasing faculty salaries there. I think they liked the fact that I knew my way around a balance sheet. This should have been my clue about the financial challenges ahead.

Soon after, I received a letter confirming the appointment, noting that "your annual salary will be $23,000, of which $4,500 will be paid to the Ohio Province." Dr. John and Sue Tew and Bud and Pat Koons gave me a typically gracious Cincinnati send-off. Dr. Earl Heine and his family, including daughters who were Trinity graduates, promised to come to my installation.

Ready for a new mission, I carried bags that were considerably heavier than they'd been when I left the convent. Gone were the despised trotters, replaced by normal shoes. Most sisters in my order now wore ordinary street clothes instead of our long, black habits. This was not because we yearned for closets full of pink and mint green. It was a practical matter.

For a hundred years, we religious had been frozen in time, living much as we had during St. Julie's era. We all got up at the same time. We ate at the same time, prayed at the same time, turned the lights out at the same time. We dressed in bulky dark robes with our hair shrouded in peculiar headgear. Some orders used what were called the disciplines, whips and chains with sharp spikes, which clasped to our biceps. The whips were small, more ceremonial than brutal, and the chains were more uncomfortable than painful. But still. And, yes, most of us shaved our heads.

Then came Vatican II. Pope John XXIII shocked the world when he announced a plan to reconsider church practices. Guided by what John XXIII called aggiornamento, or "updating," between 2,000 and 2,500 bishops and thousands of auditors, sisters, observers and secular observers convened at St. Peter's Basilica for a series of meetings from 1962 to 1965. It had been nearly 100 years since the last assembly of this kind.

Until then, Catholics didn't ask questions. Does it make sense that if you miss Mass that you will be punished forever? If a 10-year-old takes a bite of meat on Friday, is that really so serious? Why are we speaking to our flocks in Latin? Then Pope John XXIII and his successor, Pope Paul VI, officially opened the discussion. A total of sixteen elaborate documents were produced, outlining a new relationship between the church and the modern world. There were interpretations yet to be ironed out and questions to be answered.

Roman Catholic religious orders were instructed to go back and study their roots. What did your founders have in mind? What was their intent? The Sisters of Notre Dame de Namur latched on to this energetically. Hundreds of us came together to wrestle with this welcome invitation to join the modern world. We have committed our lives to the belief that education—whether it happens in a college classroom or a mud hut—offers the best hope for people in need. How would St. Julie's upbeat spirituality make itself felt today? Are there better ways to join forces with those who have resources to improve the lives of those who are suffering?

We proposed dressing in a more contemporary style, not because we had craved chic suits and bright colors but because street clothes make us more approachable. This was not a trivial decision, but one that would help us be better servants. We challenged the tradition and economics of the large convent. Maintaining a big drafty house is expensive, inconvenient and isolates us from those we serve. Some of our sisters moved to apartments and modest dwellings closer to the hospitals or schools where they worked. Our values remained the same, but we overhauled the details. We let polyester, rent and comfortable shoes into our lives.

It took some getting used to. My friend Sister Jane Roberts, who was treasurer at The Summit, jokes that when she put on her first navy blue, street-length suit she looked down in astonishment. "Oh my gosh. I still have legs." At first, we wore navy dresses and suits chosen by the order, but after a year, we were permitted to buy off the rack. I now had a modest wardrobe of long gowns, for dressy functions, and I chose one for the reception the night before my installation as president of Trinity on Dec. 8, 1975.

Entertaining Sen. Jacob Javits and Congresswoman Lindy Boggs, later U.S. Ambassador to the Holy See and mother of journalist Cokie Roberts.

The occasion was solemn and the invited guests were impressive, but times were lean and we had no business splurging on a big party. Trinity's vice president, Sister Joan Bland, approached the Belgian embassy. After all, the motherhouse of the order that owned and operated the school was located in Namur, Belgium. So the ambassador was offered the honor of hosting the elaborate reception before my installation. We also had the support of both senators from Ohio, Robert Taft Jr. and John Glenn, as well as Senators Edward Brooke, Edward Kennedy, James Buckley, Jacob Javits, Abraham Ribicoff and Lowell Weiker. Senators Howard Baker and Edmund Muskie—Trinity was friends with both sides of the aisle—were particularly charming that evening.

Maybe Dad was getting over the idea that if I joined a religious order, I would be shut away from the world. I got such a kick out of seeing him deep in conversation with Judge John Sirica, who had been named *TIME* magazine's Man of the Year for his role in the Watergate trial. Clare Booth Luce was there, looking very glamorous. Corinne (Lindy) Boggs, then a U.S. Congresswoman, was presented a Doctorate of Public Service that night. The mother of journalist Cokie Roberts, she went on to be appointed by President Bill Clinton as ambassador to the Holy See.

I assumed the mantle of president of a beautiful, historic but financially troubled institution, feeling very strongly the spirit of Trinity's founder, Sister Julia. Then leader of the Sisters of Notre Dame de Namur in the United States, she had come to Washington alone with a secret hope of founding a college. She kept her secret until she won support from Catholic University officials, America's first cardinal James Cardinal Gibbons and several influential wives of congressmen. The college opened its doors in 1900.

Early students at Trinity College were middle-class Catholic women, but in time the institution competed with Wellesley and Bryn Mawr for the daughters of the wealthy and powerful. Famous graduates of Trinity include Minority Leader of the U.S. House of Representatives Nancy Pelosi, former Secretary of Health and Human Services Kathleen Gilligan Sebelius, former chairman of Hearst Magazines Cathleen Black and many other influential business and academic leaders. As all-male colleges began to open their doors to women, they siphoned off young female graduates we'd taken for granted. We had not done enough to stem the tide.

Like our church, the college had been frozen in time. I inherited a million-dollar operating deficit and empty desks in our classrooms. I could just hear my old Summit mentor, Bud Koons. "Fill the factory." First, I had to quell a faculty rebellion, soothe dissatisfied alumni and sell something to keep the factory doors open.

At my installation, I spoke about my hopes and plans for the college and of my belief that Sister Julia Moriarty's spirit would guide me as it had my ten predesessors. And I meant it. "A viable blueprint for the future can only come from all of us, working together, the collective wisdom of all those who share responsibility," I told the crowd, which included disgruntled faculty I'd need to confront soon.

Before I arrived, the faculty had noisily voted to drop theology and philosophy from the required curriculum, which infuriated the alums. Our graduates stopped writing

Pope John Paul II on Trinity's lawn, where he greeted 300 handicapped worshippers, a move that must have driven his American Secret Service protectors crazy.

grateful checks, and they stopped sending their daughters to us. First rule of marketing 101 taught to me by my mentors on The Summit board. Look for new customers, but don't neglect the ones you already have. I was also convinced that dropping these courses was exactly the wrong idea at the wrong time.

> Barking orders has never been my style.

I steeled myself for a meeting with faculty and department heads. Even back in the days of the hot dog stand at Mount St. Joseph, I always tried to give people as many reasons as I could think of to work with me. Barking orders has never been my style. Pulling ourselves out of this financial pit together would not only be more pleasant, but faster and more effective if I leveled with them. I again drew upon what I'd learned during research for my Ph.D. The title may have been cumbersome, but the conclusion was valid. I set about trying to make the troops happy.

Alumni are angry and disappointed, I told them. Donations have dried up. We had a frank discussion of their notion of theology and philosophy. And mine. I suggested a course of study that did not revolve around worship or liturgy but would encourage critical thinking and logic, give our students solutions to modern dilemmas. Our undergraduates, I told them, should be exposed to milestones in human thought from Socrates to Aquinas to our contemporaries. Women were poised for leadership roles in every field, and as a Catholic college, Trinity could produce women with the intellectual ability to change the world to better reflect the goodness of God.

I listened. They listened. I was specific, let them know what we needed to succeed and asked for their help. They were realists, and they loved the college. Theology and philosophy were reinstated.

But strong relationships are not forged overnight or over a single issue. Margaret Durbin, who ran the physical education department, gave me a chance to prove I was still listening. And I had learned always to thank people for their help. Margaret said we needed a boat. Actually she thought we needed something called a shell, maybe four or five of them, along with oars and a crewing team. Morale is low, she said. A new sport to rally around would be good for us.

Well, I thought, it's a lot cheaper than building a gym, and the Potomac is free. Margaret was right. It was an eye opener for me to see how much enthusiasm and spirit our crewing team brought to the school. I often thought of this fledgling team later when people questioned the attention and resources Xavier University lavished on its basketball program. I thought then, and I think now, that a reason to cheer can be money well spent.

Trinity's board chairman, Pierce Flanigan Jr., who was CEO of a huge construction company in Baltimore, was my invaluable guide to best using the college's existing resources and leading me on the path to black ink. He helped us sell twenty-five acres of unused land owned by the college. The proceeds gave us breathing room to court alumni support again, and I traveled around the country to meet with them. Naturally, Sister Joan arranged for me to stay at private homes whenever possible. Free was always her favorite price.

Personal contact was important, but we also broadened our outreach, working with marketing companies, buying lists for nationwide direct-mail appeals, learning to recruit more aggressively. We added experts in diverse fields to our board of trustees, including John O'Neil, who was corporate council for General Tires, and tugboat mogul Tom Moran, and together we wiped out the deficit and established a million-dollar endowment. Enrollment increased by 47 percent and faculty salaries went up 54 percent. Students were recruited from every state and 3 percent of them came to us from foreign countries.

More money. More students. More programs. We started adult education classes and an exchange program with our sister university in Tokyo. We partnered with Washington's Hospital Center. Nursing students continued to do their clinical work at the hospital, while getting the liberal arts component for their degrees at Trinity. We ransacked the attics and closets of the school and pulled out the 75-year-old art collection, rehung it and opened a new gallery.

Two years into my presidency, Trinity received a $1 million Health Education and Welfare grant, which we used to create a special learning skills center for reading, mathematics and writing. Grant money also went toward our career development and counseling programs, and I squirreled away a wonderful cache of new ideas I would later use to help my students at Xavier.

New ideas were built on a foundation of tradition, carefully translated by Sister Helen Sheehan. Trinity's institutional memory and a loyal and discreet adviser, Sister Helen could make herself nearly invisible, listening quietly from the edge of my office or from the back row of a faculty meeting. Overnight, she'd run a problem through the prism of her encyclopedic memory. The next day in the quiet of my office or the dining room or even trailing me out the front steps of the Main Hall, she would deliver a gem.

In her soft voice with curious undertones of eastern sophistication—sort of Jackie Kennedy-esque—she would come up with a shrewd, resourceful idea. Funding, approaches to alumnae, property sales, faculty snits, curriculum changes—she had perspective, context, history.

"I know you are concerned," she would begin diffidently, "and I thought you might want some background." I did. She was often the author of a solution to what had seemed to be a hopeless impasse.

Semi-retired when I arrived, she spent hours next to the paid receptionist, our ambassador at the front door of the Great Hall. She was particularly fond of my father, who visited once a month or so. She always made sure the master guest room on the front corridor was ready for him, and she fussed over me. "Eat, eat, eat," she'd plead, as time went by and the workload seem to pare flesh from my bones. Everyone loved Sister Helen. Few could pass her without giving her a hug. She was there when I came and there when I left. Some years later, I read of her passing. I imagine new legions of faculty and students and their families bestowing hugs on this marvelous woman. I will imagine one of those hugs was from me.

Despite the rigors of the job, I began to enjoy my new life at Trinity. I looked forward to the bi-annual trip to Cape Cod, where many alumnae had homes. One woman had a rambling house near the Kennedy compound at Hyannis Port, and hundreds of Trinity graduates would converge, exchanging memories and craning our necks toward the six acres of waterfront and the white frame clapboard buildings where the first Catholic President of the United States had vacationed. I was never so overcome by reverence for the surroundings that I did not make a strong pitch for money before the alumnae climbed back in their big cars and headed back to Maryland or Maine, Virginia or Vermont.

At The Summit, I had taken up running, which became part of my daily routine in Washington, and I loved biking around the campus. Rehoboth Beach in Delaware with its stretches of sandy beach was only a couple of hours away. Then Pope John Paul II announced he was coming to Trinity in October of 1979, which put a crimp in lobster fishing and sailing that summer.

There was a flurry of preparation, protocol and general sprucing up, but I didn't mind because I think choosing our school as a destination was his quiet way of recognizing the importance of the Church's women. In Trinity's Notre Dame Chapel,

His Holiness led an ecumenical prayer service with leaders of Protestant, Eastern Orthodox, Jewish and other non-Christian religions, something that would never have happened before Vatican II.

Arriving about ninety minutes late, having given three major addresses that morning—one to religious women, one to educators and one to students at Catholic University—he emerged from a black limousine. He focused full attention on me as I gave my three-minute welcome speech, in spite of the physical pressure of the crowds against our ribs and the din of their shouts in our ears. I remember clearly his piercing, unwavering, kindly eyes and the punctuation of his thumb on the palm of my hand, which he held throughout my greeting.

This pope was easy to work with, gentle and undemanding. He did have one request, which must have driven his American Secret Service detail crazy. He wanted to meet with crippled children of the Washington Archdiocese. Word got around, and the campus filled with gravely afflicted people of all ages. Hundreds of them on gurneys, in wheelchairs, on crutches. The pope moved slowly through the Kerby Hall lawn, greeting every one of them, touching them, blessing them, bending down to hug the little ones.

After that, the last big occasion for me in our nation's capital was the inauguration of Ronald Reagan in 1981. As the new president was giving his inaugural address, fifty-two American hostages in Iran were released after more than a year in captivity, and the national Christmas tree on the ellipse near the White House was re-lighted in celebration. That night, there were glittery inaugural balls, which I attended with presidents of nearby colleges and universities including Catholic University, Georgetown, Gallaudet, American, George Washington and Howard. We were greeted by the President and his wife. It was very heady, and I was flattered to be invited.

Back on campus, I was meeting with students one Friday a month. Sometimes I'd have a casual agenda. After they got to know me better, they came up with ideas and agendas of their own. Of course, I talked to a lot of students informally as I roamed the campus, but I thought it was important to set up these regular sessions to make sure I never lost touch with them. It's easy to look up from a mound of papers in your corner office and realize that you haven't seen a real live student in weeks.

Trying not to sound preachy, I talked about service to others and the wise use of power. I knew these women were heading out into a world where they could have enormous impact—much more so than the previous generation. Trinity's new master's degree programs in teaching and business administration recognized a marketplace where they would be making the rules, not simply carrying out the orders of others.

Sister Mary Ann Cook, Trinity's academic dean, wrote:

"As women awaken to new options of lifestyle and career and to the injustice of lingering discrimination, they find themselves courted by employers desperate to satisfy affirmative action regulations. Liberal arts colleges for women have a special responsibility to teach the whole range of disciplines rooted in a sense of values and goals. Otherwise, we may release women from typewriters only to chain them to computers."

Trinity's Honor Code, which existed at the campus since 1913, challenged these young women to act honorably and honestly, whether or not anybody is looking. A wonderful notion—policing ourselves. Knowing there is right and wrong, good and bad and deciding for ourselves to do right and good. Every time we make these good choices for ourselves, I believe it becomes easier, more certain.

There have been times at Xavier—not a lot, but some—when I have learned of cheating in class. In every instance that I recall, the students confessed to me. They had dipped a toe in the honor system. I wanted them to take the plunge. My advice was always to go back to the faculty member, own up and ask for an F. I would not do it for them.

It was not easy for them. But it was right, and they knew it in their hearts. I believe the lesson followed them, informing decisions they would make later in life.

When I left Trinity, I clutched Sister Julia's favorite scripture to my heart. "Not to us, oh, Lord, not to us but to your name give glory," a spirit caught by thousands of students and spread to various parts of this country and the international community. I was deeply moved by the tradition of the honor system, which taught students to weigh their personal desires against the greater good. Learning trust based on love and respect for the rights of others can last a lifetime and color everything we do.

I don't think it's a stretch to believe this translates to something that is very dear, in fact essential, to athletes. Team players have to completely trust each other and develop a sense of selflessness. They have to pass the ball. If you're a defender and the opposing team sets up a screen that keeps you from following your man, you have to know another teammate will pick him up. Honor. Trust. Teamwork. I believe with every day and every lesson learned, I was inching closer to understanding my life's work. I didn't know what God had planned for me next, but I knew my years at Trinity had been another piece of the puzzle.

And I was blessed to be invited.

4

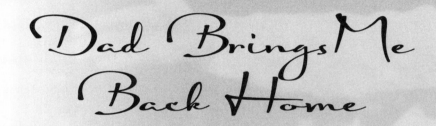

Dad Brings Me Back Home

At peace with my Ignatian surroundings and curious
about the lives of the university's complicated students.

*T*he news from Cincinnati was ominous. Dad was not well.

My smart, methodical, loyal father was not himself. He was confused. He would start the car and forget where he was going. He'd leave the stove on. My brother, Tom, said I was too skinny, was working too hard and, besides, Dad needed me. It was time to come home.

The phone rang almost before I had unpacked my bags. After making arrangements with the college and clearing it with my order, I took some time to unwind and was returning to live at the convent where I had taken my vows. Father Charles Currie, whom I'd met at Trinity, was on the line. Charlie had just been named president of Xavier University, and through an academic or Catholic grapevine, he had heard I was back in Cincinnati and wanted me to work for him.

Charismatic and decisive, he set about organizing my life. I wanted my MBA, I told him. And I thought a law degree would be handy. Oh, well, that's easy, he said. You can teach a couple of classes and get your MBA at Xavier. A wonderful program there, he said. Wonderful. Nearby Chase College of Law across the river in northern Kentucky would be convenient. He'd already set up an interview with the dean at Xavier. Two classes in English. You'll love it. It'll be great.

Although Xavier University is a Jesuit school and my entire religious life, beginning at The Summit, had been committed to a different religious order, scholars had charted similarities between St. Julie Billiart and Jesuit founder St. Ignatius of Loyola. Both revered education and led their followers toward both the intellectual and the spiritual. I liked the idea of returning to the classroom. It had been far too long, and I realized that I missed teaching. A lot. I was given the okay from my order, and off I went.

It was 1982 and the beginning of a new life for me, one I'd never have imagined. As I look back, I can see all the pieces of the puzzle were about to fall into place. Tom even said I was putting back on the weight I'd lost in Washington. I felt at peace with my Ignatian surroundings, and I loved my students.

From the beginning, I found myself drawn to the athletes in my classes. Most of them led complicated lives. One young man was a soccer player who carried a full load of classes and worked nights at the campus radio station. His family, recent immigrants from South America, lived in Boston. His sports scholarship didn't cover all his expenses, and his family didn't have the money to help. Somehow, he managed on the soccer field, at work and in class, always prepared for my questions. Another good student was a swimmer who always arrived at class with her long, blond hair dripping from practice at the pool. Waving her hand wildly, she knew the answers almost before I asked the questions. Another girl, a volleyball player, often showed up with an ice pack on her shoulder.

> **This 18-year-old from a rough New York City neighborhood did a very brave thing. He trusted me with the truth.**

They had obligations and pressures far beyond those of my other students. I admired them and said so when their coaches checked in with me. All the coaches I was getting to know at Xavier kept an eye on their players' classroom performance. Some of it, of course, was self interest. If their athletes' grades weren't up to snuff, they couldn't play, couldn't help win games. But most coaches at Xavier looked out for their players' lives off the field and beyond the college campus. It was an everyday, working example of the Cura Personalis, the Jesuit mantra of serving and caring for the whole person.

One student, in this same first-semester English class, would try our resolve.

*D*onnie was like a camel in reverse. He just couldn't get enough water. Every day it was the same. About ten minutes into the class, he would saunter to the the head of the class, stand in front of me, politely tell me he needed a drink and then walk out the door. The water fountain was just outside, so the first time, I expected him to be right back. He wasn't. The class was only fifty minutes long, and Donnie routinely spent a third of it slaking his thirst.

An assistant to then-head basketball coach Bob Staak called to see how Donnie was doing. Well, I told him, I'm afraid Donnie is dehydrated. Can you send a bottle of water with him to class? The coach was shocked. What the...?! In deference to my vocation, he never finished the sentence, but, like magic, the water breaks stopped.

Clearly, water wasn't the problem. I asked Donnie to stay after class. I could see that he was angry, but I plowed ahead, smiling and cheerful, trying to look as friendly as if I were Sister Mary Constance outside the principal's office at Mt. Notre Dame High School. And this 18-year-old from a rough New York City neighborhood did a very brave thing. He trusted me with the truth.

He told me he left class because he was afraid I would call on him, and he wouldn't know the answer.

Richie Harris—laying the foundation.

I asked if he really wanted to learn, and he insisted that he did. I said I would help him. We had a lot of work to do. An exceptional athlete, he had never been pressed to write a paper, never been expected to pass a test. His specialty was basketball, not books. Now his life had changed in a threatening and humiliating way. He still had the jump shot, but he lacked basic classroom skills and nobody was looking the other way. He could lose everything.

I told him I'd make a deal. If he came to my office twice a week at 7 a.m., I'd help, tutoring him on the basics most of my other students had been taught in high school. He was never, ever late. And he never, ever missed a morning. We would go over the material for the week, then I would send him out to breakfast while I went to Bellarmine Chapel for Mass. We'd meet again at 9:30.

He started putting his hand up in class, competing with the swimmer to spout the right answers. From time to time, his mother would call, excited about his progress and asking if she could do anything to help. "Just love him and encourage him," I said. "We'll do our best to help him with the rest." Our best turned out not to be good enough. He passed my English class, and I couldn't wait to tell his mother. Then Donnie disappeared.

Classes had been dismissed for the Christmas holiday, but when his mother went to pick him up at the airport, he didn't get off the plane. Panicky, she called the athletics department, and they called me. "Check with the other players," I told them. "Somebody knows." Meanwhile, I discovered he had been having trouble with his other classes. He couldn't face his mother with the news, so he had slipped off to Kentucky for the holidays with a friend.

He knew failing grades meant he couldn't play basketball, a treasured success in his young life. In fact, he was such an outstanding player that the newspapers in Cincinnati were clamoring for details about why he was benched. He had not only failed, but he was failing publicly. I was beginning to understand the tremendous pressure these athletes faced. And how much help they truly needed.

I also was seeing first-hand why Bill Daily was smart to hire Bob Staak.

Xavier University, which had not fielded a football team since 1973, had pinned its hopes on basketball. Bill Daily was president of Xavier's Athletics Board from 1975 to 1984, while the university was mired in defeat. Bill played basketball for XU as a freshman and had later coached and was on the communications faculty. Although he's a very nice guy, he did not like the idea of finishing last. He went searching for somebody who could win.

"I had enough knowledge and experience to be ignorant," Bill says with typical self-deprecation. He went to UCLA's legendary coach John Wooden. "He didn't give me any names, but he told me what we should look for." Among other things, Wooden told them to look for a "strong family man" because of the stress of the job.

"So we asked a lot of personal questions as well as questions about athletics," he says. "We had about fifty questions and we took everybody through the same process." From a list of forty-five candidates, they winnowed the choice down to five men, including a University of Pennsylvania assistant coach named Staak. "I started following him around, going to games, watching how he interacted with the players. I really liked him. He was loud, dynamic, smoked cigars."

The sky was spitting a nasty mix of sleet and snow when Bill picked Bob Staak up in a blue Volkswagen Beetle for his interview with the selection committee. Old VW Bugs were notorious for wheezing heaters and defrosters. A student in the backseat and Bob in the passenger seat tried gamely to keep ahead of the sleet on the windows, scraping with pieces of cardboard and shreds of paper. "It was a miserable day, but we took him to Dockside VI in Norwood. He ate two bowls of their clam chowder and forgave Cincinnati."

On the way to the meeting, Bill kept making Coach Staak practice not saying "Egg-savier." At the basketball game later, "There were only about three hundred in the stands. I think Bob had every confidence he could do better."

Coach Staak, head coach at Xavier from 1979 to 1985, recruited all-state players, fired up the fans, moved home games from Schmidt Memorial Field House to the Cincinnati Gardens and upgraded the schedule to almost all Division I teams. It was a spectacular turnaround. He had a knack for winning and a knack for spotting talent.

"We went looking for a recruiter who could coach," Bill remembers.

Bob brought in several members of the Xavier University 1,000 Point Club, including Byron Larkin, Anthony Hicks, Jeff Jenkins, Dexter Bailey, Richie Harris and Victor Fleming.

Richie Harris, one of the best players in the state of New York as a high school senior, says he was approached by three hundred colleges. Assistant XU coach Wayne Morgan, later Iowa State's first African American coach, and Bob Staak came calling. "They were the only ones who talked about transformation," Richie says. "And at first all they talked to me about was academics. Then it was, 'oh by the way, you can help lay the foundation for a great basketball program.' They couldn't say 'we won this or we won that.' Because they hadn't. They were selling possibilities, a dream. I think they knew this was exactly the right lure for me."

Bob Staak and his recruiters were tenacious and smart. Once Bob found what he wanted, he wouldn't let go. Just then, he wanted Donnie back, and he wanted him eligible to play ball. The rest of us were willing allies.

A couple of Coach Staak's assistants went to Kentucky to retrieve Donnie and put him on a plane home. He returned to campus early the next semester, even though he was not allowed to play right away. He was determined to get back on the team and ready to earn a college degree. He had promised his mother.

"Listen," I said, "you passed my class. I didn't give you any breaks. You did the work, the same as everybody else. Now you know you can get the grades. You have the ability to be a good student. Let's work on your other classes."

I helped him personally, but I also set him up with tutors for his other subjects. Bright and committed, he had a lot going for him He was a fixture at study hall and learned how to take good notes in class, a new skill. He buckled down and studied. If he didn't understand something, he said so. He was surrounded by people with answers. He became eligible the next semester and played for the Musketeers alongside great players such as Byron Larkin.

At the annual sports banquet his senior year, Donnie came up to the microphone. Now, this was the guy who used to pretend to use the drinking fountain so he wouldn't have to talk in class. He began by saying he wanted to give glory to God for the gifts he had been given, especially the gift of being able to play basketball.

Bob Staak led a spectacular turnaround for Xavier basketball after Bill Daily taught him not to say "Eggs-savier."

I was not surprised. Our best student-athletes seem to be keenly aware that they have been singled out and blessed with tremendous skills and special talents. They know not many people can do what they do, and despite what we hear about spoiled jocks, I have seen them carry their gifts with tremendous humility.

But here is the stunning part: Donnie said he was grateful to play basketball so he could earn a Xavier degree—not the other way around. This was a huge moment for me. The National Basketball Association (NBA), as it turned out, was not to be his meal ticket. He was not drafted, but he had other options and a college degree that would make his plans possible. He went back to the inner city as a social worker.

Nearly ten years later, I was on the road with the team in Philadelphia when a tall, well-dressed man approached me in the hotel dining room. I recognized Donnie right away. He looked great, smiling and still boyish. After five years in social services, specializing in cases involving children, he went to work for General Electric while he went back to school studying computer technology and information systems. Now a consultant, he works in Florida. He thanked me, said I had changed his life.

Well, he changed mine for thirty years after I met him. From the moment I started our early morning sessions, I didn't need a little white envelope to know what my mission would be: putting more Donnies in caps and gowns.

He taught me when we run into someone who doesn't appear to want to learn, we have to find out why. Sometimes it's because they can't learn the way we're teaching. Some can't learn from listening to a lecture. Others have trouble processing the written word. Sometimes they're just overwhelmed. Or under-challenged. One size hardly ever fits all. Mario Montessori reminded us at The Summit about his mother's method of finding each child's unique style of learning and, more than that, assuming everyone wants to learn.

Standing there in a business suit was a person who embodied our goal at Xavier— growth through physical, cognitive, social, emotional and spiritual means. The whole package. The whole person. I think of all the people in his life there—his coaches and the players, for sure, plus plenty of tutors, teachers and advisers. His mother's love and prodding were also essential. This young man fought hard for an education, then turned around to share it with kids whose struggles he understood. Was that a kind of self-imposed internship? A return on the investment in him? I'm guessing it might have been.

Imagine what we'd have squandered if he'd been thrown out of school because this jock had bad grades and spent too much time at the water fountain.

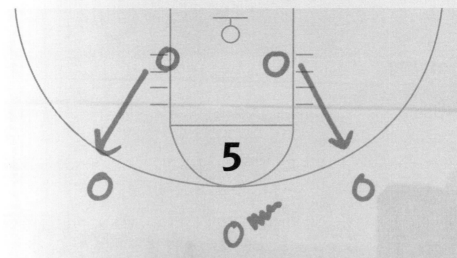

5

Making it Official

To connect with athletes, I had to know something about the game. Pointers from Brian Grant (left) and Erik Edwards.

$\mathcal{D}$oris Jackson has an easy laugh, an informed heart and a head for organization. Add to that a fierce work ethic. Xavier University was lucky to have found her, and I was lucky to have found myself in the office next to her. Maybe I have good desk karma. We met when I started working with Donnie in the mornings. Our doors were open, and she could hear what we were doing. I was not only tutoring Donnie in English, but I was on the phone to his teachers to see how he was faring in his other subjects.

Most teachers have enough on their plates teaching students already prepared to learn, with the fundamental skills you'd expect from a high school graduate. They don't have much time for remedial lessons, but everybody has an ego, and I was careful to tread lightly. I was not trying to take over anybody's job or tell him how to run his classroom. I was as respectful as I know how to be, but I was persistent. I took a lot of pride in building a network of teachers and tutors who could propel Donnie toward his degree.

Doris would say later that she liked what she was hearing. Like me, she was fairly new to Xavier. Her title was director of academic advising, a new program the university had hired her to build from scratch, a huge undertaking. To complicate matters, things were heating up in the world of college athletics and academics.

Mike Fish, senior writer for *Sports Illustrated*, wrote:

"The cash handshake. The phony grades. Cover-ups and the athletics folks looking the other way. This is the dirty stuff about college sports that won't be found in one of those public service announcements created by the good folks at NCAA headquarters."

No whiff of "the dirty stuff" had attached itself to Xavier, and the new athletics director, Jeff Fogelson, planned to keep it that way. Men's basketball is the alpha sport. It's the rallying point for students, a chance for national recognition, the university's brand.

We all knew that the competition was turning up a notch, for coaching staff, for wins and, of course, for players. Jeff was put in charge of the whole thing, and Xavier President Charlie Currie couldn't have made a better choice. Not only an able administrator, he was honorable and decent. Jeff and I were acquainted from my time in Washington, when he was on the student affairs staff at Georgetown. He pushed Xavier's administration for an academic program exclusively for athletes. It wasn't a hard sell.

A mission statement came from the office of the president:

"Consistent with the Jesuit philosophy of education and mission of the University, the Xavier University intercollegiate athletics program strives to enhance and integrate the intellectual, moral, spiritual, emotional, social and physical growth of young men and women. Each sport operates in an environment of integrity and ethical conduct which promotes academic success, fiscal responsibility, competitive excellence, sportsmanship, community service and equitable opportunities for all students and staff, including women and minorities."

Apparently these Jesuits were serious.

> "I knew some players on campus were laughing about being sent to a nun. Some alumni weren't convinced either.

Father Currie had seen the successful partnership in the 1970s at Georgetown between head basketball coach John Thompson and academic coordinator Mary Fenlon. "I wanted something like that at Xavier, and I thought Rose Ann would be ideal," says Father Currie, who today collaborates on an international effort to connect refugees with educational opportunities. "She had exceptional qualifications and, in my opinion, the right temperament. She succeeded beyond my hopes."

Jeff met with Doris, and she and I were on our way to a decades long partnership. In August 1985, the position of coordinator of academic athletics advising was created, and I was appointed. Specifically, Jeff asked me to work with men's basketball first, women's basketball second, then any other athlete who needed me if I had time left over. Doris was at the top of my organizational chart, not the athletics director. Jeff himself emphasized this: Education is the assignment, the top priority. Your duty is to the student, not the team. It never occurred to me that it would be any other way.

Coaches were not permitted to contact professors directly. I was to be the link between athletics and academics. Pete Gillen would later grant me what is widely known as the "benching" privilege. But right from the beginning, I was given the "snooping" privilege. My assignment was to wade knee deep into the student athlete's test scores and class performance. "We know she knows the deal on each of us," Byron Larkin would say as an undergraduate.

There was no budget at first and not everybody was as enthusiastic as Jeff, Doris and I were. I knew some players on campus were laughing about being sent to a nun. Some alumni weren't convinced either. "It is pitiful to read that Xavier has engaged a nun to coax and beg its basketball players to pass their courses," wrote one in a letter to a local newspaper. "What utter nonsense... Think of it. Xavier employs a nun armed with a degree in law as well as advanced degrees in business, literature and education to serve as a combined babysitter and house mother for the dullards on its basketball team who would otherwise fail... As a graduate of Xavier, I am embarrassed."

When I would tell people from other universities about my assignment, they'd often ask, "Is that a full time job?" I didn't say so, but it was full time and then some.

I was literally living and breathing Xavier University. After I began teaching and studying for my MBA, I usually returned home to the convent after everybody else was in bed. The kitchen was closed, and there was nothing to eat. Not for the first time, I was thankful for Vatican II. I was allowed to move into the Manor House, small apartments with kitchens built for married graduate students on Victory Parkway at the edge of campus. My tiny place cost $395 a month, which I probably saved in gasoline.

Dad had moved to a nursing home just over the Ohio River in Ft. Thomas, Kentucky, and I drove over to see him nearly every day. From the window of Dad's room was a view of the hillside Cincinnati neighborhood of Mt. Adams, where he'd grown up. Tom said he hoped that might give him pleasure, but my father's lucid moments were numbered. Aunt Mary had died while I was still at The Summit of complications from a minor surgery. It fell to Tom and Theresa to bring us together for holidays. Sister Jane Roberts was pulled into the family circle—Aunt Jane to Tom and Theresa's five children.

I was in class in 1983 when word reached me of Dad's death. Our time together over the years had allayed his doubts about the choice I had made, and I think it put his heart at ease. His last words to me were, "Mary, what a wonderful woman. Oh, Mary. Boy, could she cook." Was he talking about my mother, Mary Gertrude? Or Mary Cecelia, his sister who had helped raise his children? Or both? No matter. The answer is that he was a traditional and loving family man to the end.

After Dad died, I felt a bit adrift. I roamed the campus, spending as much time with my students as I could. My day was full. Up at 4 a.m. First, meditation and prayer, then exercise. I used to run every morning before working with free weights. Now, on cold and snowy days, I sometimes use my new elliptical machine which gobbles up precious space in my little room. I still work out with free weights, and I feel great, don't have any aches or pains.

Nearly a year ago, while I was speaking to an alumni group at Cincinnati Country Club, I experienced what was called a transient ischemic attack (TIA), a momentary loss of blood to the brain. The audience was loaded with medical experts and concerned friends.

I was whisked off for a series of tests and pronounced fit. No damage, no treatment, no predictors, except my age. I think it falls under the category of "just one of those things."

Some people seem to think I'm skinny, an observation most everybody is willing to make in a way they don't about women who are, shall we say, not skinny. I weigh 112 pounds and am five feet, four inches tall. According to the Internet, I'm on the low end of the chart for my height, weight and frame. And, good luck Googling this without pawing your way through sneaky ads for Garcinia Cambogia and offers to make friends with Jenny Craig.

Myers-Briggs testing in 2001 found that I am am an extroverted, intuitive, thinking, judging type. The report gave me the Field Marshall label, a person who "cannot not lead." People who are like me, according to the psychologists, need positive feedback and an absence of routine. We function best when we have mental challenges and interesting problems to solve.

I can operate an automobile in good standing, including the vision test, and I do not wear eye glasses or contact lenses. I exercise every single day, even on the road. Doris Jackson used to worry when we were in a strange town because I would throw on my track suit and run no matter where we were—even in sketchy neighborhoods. Now, just about every hotel has an exercise room and some have a pool. No excuses, even if I wanted one. If I get the choice between french fries and a green salad, I pick the salad every time. I do not drink alcohol, and I do not look down my nose at those who do.

I attend Mass every morning at 8 a.m. at Bellarmine Chapel on Xavier's campus and pray many times during the day, but not about my health.

My living arrangements have made me more available to my students, and they are more available to me. I have been known to pound on the door of a student who has trouble getting to class. We bump into each other as neighbors, giving me the chance to know them in casual and unguarded moments, and I spend time with their families as well, attending birthdays, weddings and funerals whenever I am invited. I learned long ago that it is easier to do something hard when you're asked by someone you like. And five minutes with a young man's chatty sister can save five hours of trying to figure out what makes him tick.

"If you stay out of her dog house, she's actually a real sweet person," a student-athlete told a *Cincinnati Magazine* reporter. I'm a big believer in the power of conversation. I'm a good listener, but I also talk a lot. I never had any problem with vows of chastity and poverty, but I don't think I could have taken one of silence.

Of course, to really connect with the athletes, I had to know something about their game.

I watched them practice, watched them compete at home and traveled with them to away games. Some players probably weren't that thrilled to see me. Kenny Harvey, a shooting guard who graduated in 1997, claims I thought nothing of settling in beside him on the bus or plane, pulling his earphones off his head and handing him an outline of what he needed to finish while he was on the road. He played behind Lenny Brown, and he didn't get as much playing time as he wanted. But he never grumbled and never missed practice. Movie-star handsome, he's a financial manager in Chicago with a similarly handsome family and the same great smile.

Traveling with the team was never an excuse not to do the assignment. I set up on-the-road study tables in hotels and in drafty arenas. I started going to the locker room after every game. Our basketball players always knelt down after a game, holding a teammate's hand while they said The Lord's Prayer together before the coach talked to them.

Over the years, I've learned a lot about basketball. I know the basics of setting a screen to block a defender. I know what double-teaming is. I know the difference between man-on-man versus zone defense. I understand all that, and I certainly understand the nature of competition. But, as much as I learned to appreciate the game they were playing, it was the means to an end. I am part of a deal between the university and its athletes, and I don't mind saying that I always tried to see if I could get the athletes the best of the bargain.

I shared their lives, and I got them to share mine. Some of them started coming around to my office, just hanging out. I was glad they did for so many reasons. First of all, I genuinely liked the players. But, second, it was important that my office was not seen as a place where just "dumb jocks" went to pull their grades up. When men like Byron Larkin or Richie Harris came to visit, it was peer pressure of the very best kind. It was evidence that the academic advising office is not a bad place to be. Or, as Yogi Berra put it: "You can observe a lot just by watching."

Byron was a natural leader, who grew up in Cincinnati and played ball for Moeller High School. I think Bob Staak could be tough on him. Coach was gruff, loud and swore a lot. Maybe I represented the sympathetic voice after a visit to the principal's office. At six-foot-three, he was not big by national basketball standards and instead played six seasons abroad after graduation. Byron was the first player in Xavier history to lead the team in scoring four straight years. He also might have been the first player to come to my office who didn't need help in the classroom.

If Byron was first, Richie Harris was hard on his heels.

Every time Richie showed up at my office, he wore a pin-striped suit, crisp shirt and tie. Dressed for the job, he said. He was interning at Franklin Saving & Loan while he was playing ball. His grades were good, and I wondered how he managed. "Discipline," he said. "I have discipline." Recruited from New York, he said a scholarship to military school had not only taught him how to study and, as he put it, he had learned to take time out to learn. "Taking time out to learn" became my mantra.

A 1986 graduate, he was captain three out of the four years he played for us. "Although I was quiet, I think I could set the pace off the court too," Richie says. "Keeping the players eligible wasn't just Sister's job. It was up to everybody who could help. I thought of myself as one of her unintended assistants." When I first talked to Richie about studying and scheduling and career, he told me gently that these were things he had already thought about. "I was already committed to getting the most out of school," he says.

Another smart young man who used to come around my office a lot was Michael Davenport.

"Even back then, when she was just kind of new to the university, Sister Fleming was a big deal. She was front and center in their recruiting efforts. And she stuck with us when we got to campus. Boy, did she ever. She was always checking to make sure we were in class."

He says some of the players started sitting along the sides of the classroom, where they might not be seen from a casual glance inside the room from the doorway. They could insist they were there, but maybe Sister just didn't see them.

"Didn't work," Michael says. "She'd throw open the door and look over the whole classroom. She knew if you were there." Or if you weren't.

Michael was never a problem. From the beginning, I thought Michael could do about anything he wanted. He had a wide range of interests, including cooking, and he was excited about the prospect of studying in Spain for a semester. His scholarship to Xavier would cover all his living expenses there, plus the tuition and books. We'd even

Michael Davenport, a bank executive, says being a good athlete is like winning the lottery but being one who can play in the pros is "winning the lottery and the kicker."

found a place for him to work out, so he wouldn't get fat on the Spanish food he loved. We were allowed to pay for everything except the ticket to get there and back.

Paying his travel expenses would have violated National Collegiate Athletic Association (NCAA) rules, and he didn't have enough money to pay for it himself. I understand that there were reasons for restricting the money that could be given to athletes. We kept the team locker room locked during games because of rumors about boosters at other schools slipping hundred-dollar bills into the players' sneakers. College sports was still rife with recruiting violations and improper benefits.

We all tried to figure out a way to get Michael on a plane to Spain that would not violate either the letter or the intent of the rule. We failed. But he didn't sulk. He didn't call a press conference. He didn't consult an attorney. He continued to give the university its money's worth and then some. Today, he says he barely remembers the episode.

He says his father always discouraged what he called "shoulda woulda coulda" talk. "It's not what might have happened, it's what you do with your life," Michael says.

He was co-captain on the team his junior and senior seasons and the team's leading scorer his senior year before he was injured. After graduating in 1991 with more than 1,000 points earned on the court for Xavier, Michael Davenport headed for the pros. But at the tryout in Wichita, Kansas, the coach cut the guy from Xavier, because in Wichita, they told him, only players from Kansas State bring in the fans.

"That was the first time I had ever gotten cut from any team. Any team," he says. After a time, he realized he was spiraling into a depression. "I didn't know it at first. My hair was falling out. I wasn't exercising, and I was still eating that large pizza." He laughs. "The dryer was shrinking my clothes."

He was dealing with a death, he says, "the death of a dream."

Being a really good athlete, he says, is like "winning the lottery." A college education. Lots of attention. But being a really, really good athlete, one who can play in the pros is "winning the lottery and the kicker." He was surrounded by people who were convinced of his worth off the court, "my mom, my grandmother, my dad, my wife—people who brought truth into my life."

Michael graciously said he could see Wichita made a good business decision. The man who played under Pete Gillen on the first Xavier squad to go to the NCAA Sweet 16 was smart enough to realize his playing days were over.

This time, the system worked the way it is supposed to. Michael Davenport played hard for Xavier, but his education and degree from the university would prepare him to use his considerable talents elsewhere. He had options. He earned a law degree from the University of Cincinnati, worked as an assistant basketball coach at West Point and Xavier, and landed at U.S. Bank in Cincinnati. Starting as a branch manager, he worked his way up to vice president, staying abreast of federal banking regulations. Now, he's at First Financial, heading up the bank's operational and regulatory risk department.

> Getting these students to respect the clock was probably one of the best things we've ever done for them.

He knows better than most about playing by complicated and fluid rules.

I was always happy to see the players at my office, but it was cramped. We needed more space and a bigger table. I started a study hall for athletes. Really just a couple of tables at the library, it was the beginning of structure they needed. I ran it myself for a while, then I put Mae Faggs Starr in charge, an athlete with immediate credibility with my students. Plus she drove a very impressive Cadillac. A two-time Olympic medal winner in field and track, she was a champion in every way you can imagine, shrugging off the racism of the '50s to thrive at college in Tennessee and mentoring Olympic great Wilma Rudolph, considered the fastest woman in the world in the 1960s. She received a master's degree from the University of Cincinnati and then taught physical education at high schools in the Cincinnati area.

While tending the study hall, she knitted constantly. When she finished a colorful afghan, she'd put players' names in a hat and draw a winner.

Our students loved her.

Mae hired some upperclassmen to help with tutoring, and one night a week I taught a workshop in study skills and time management. Getting these students to respect the clock was probably one of the best things we've ever done for them. Their coaches certainly appreciated it. Practice started at 3 p.m., and they had little patience with a player who was still lacing up his shoes at 3:05. I like to think I might have been responsible for some of them showing up on time in later life to job interviews.

After the program matured and we were getting attention for our academic success, sports agents began to call me about specific players they thought might be headed for the National Basketball Association (NBA). They ask about personal character. They want to know about an athlete's personal integrity, his commitment to hard work and his willingness to take direction and be coached. I don't keep track of their three pointers, but I know their personalities inside out.

Richie Harris was a good basketball player and a good student, and, even better, was grateful for his gifts. Like Donnie, Richie reached out to life beyond the basketball court, working with young people through a local orphanage and Shining Star Sports. He'd also come back during the summer to tutor players in the Summer Bridge Program. He was a marvelous role model, reaching kids who might not have been as open to the message from somebody else. He worked as a volunteer, free of charge. Richie called it "putting cookies back in the cookie jar."

I have read the writings of high minded scholars who couldn't have put it better.

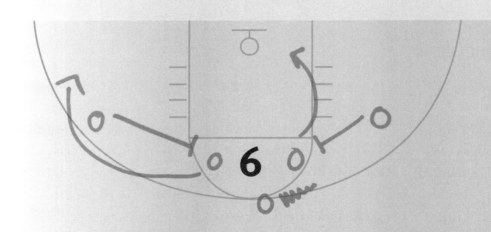

Pete Gillen
and the Bench

Pete Gillen shared the power.

*P*ete Gillen was back on Xavier's campus, this time as an observer. Still boyish with thick coppery hair and a grin on his ruddy face, he didn't look much different than he did in 1985 when he was head coach for men's basketball. Now a sportscaster for CBS, his Brooklyn syntax is blunted but not entirely subdued. And he flings around similes and mixes metaphors with wild abandon.

"I thought she would be a fish out of water, but I was wrong," Pete said of me to a reporter, adding, "Nobody's in the same ballpark with her."

Not that he didn't have his doubts at first about my ability to deal with his players. "They're young, they mostly haven't had authority figures in their lives, and they cut corners as easily as they breathe. They're going to buffalo you." As I said, wild abandon. He's a walking sound bite. After a losing game: "We were like a bakery. It was apple, cherry, whatever type of turnover you want, we had 'em."

I liked Pete right from the beginning. Not only did he make me laugh, but I admired his character and his concern for his players. He and his wife, Ginny, a good cook, occasionally invited the team over to their house for dinner. Not only was the food great, but they set their table with beautiful crystal, silver and china. He showed the young players respect. He invited me one night with a warning. "There's going to be a guy there who's mad at us," he said.

"Me too?" I said, surprised.

"Yeah," he answered. "He played ball for us, and he never graduated. He will attack you."

Well, who could resist an invitation like that?

Pete was right. The young man felt exploited and abandoned. His basketball days with Xavier were finished, and he had no degree to show for it. He was working at a fast-food chain, not making much money. He said his supervisor liked him and thought he had a future, but he needed a degree to be considered for the management program. The cost of tuition, he said, was out of his reach. The young man did play for Xavier, but it was before Pete Gillen had even arrived on campus.

> Simply buffing up a grade to manipulate the system, play until the institution gets what it wants is wrong.

We talked for a while, then I went back to the office and pulled his records. He was twelve credits short of graduation, and I told Pete I thought with some help, he could do the work and earn a degree.

Pete got the money somewhere. For all I know, he and Ginny paid for it.

The young man graduated.

Whenever he gets a chance to talk about Xavier, Pete always is generous with praise for his predecessor, Bob Staak. "I didn't want to start at ground zero," Pete says. "I wanted to win some games right away, and Bob had done a terrific job with Xavier's team. He built it. I doubt I ever would have taken the job at Xavier if Bob hadn't done what he did."

What Bob did was turn Xavier into a winning team and lay the foundation for the program today. In 1981, the men's basketball team compiled an 8–3 Midwestern City Conference (MCC) record and captured its first league title. Two years later, Xavier captured its first MCC Tournament Championship and its first NCAA berth since 1961. Coach Staak then led the team back to the National Invitational Tournament (NIT) in 1984 for the first time since the 1958 championship. And his prowess went beyond men's basketball. For a time, he handled the dual role of athletics director and coach. As AD, Bob Staak led the Musketeers into conference play in all men's sports in 1979 and moved the women into the North Star Conference in 1983, helped by the new assistant athletics director Jeff Fogelson.

Charlie Currie hired Jeff to assume some of Coach Staak's workload then quickly promoted him to athletics director. Besides a good mind and expansive knowledge of sports, Jeff brought a welcome camaraderie to the athletics department. Wiry with a dry sense of humor, he was modest about his own accomplishments but bragged profusely about his wife, Nancy, who taught children with special needs in some of Cincinnati's poorest neighborhoods.

Jeff started a tradition of potluck New Year's Eve gatherings at his home, giving those of us in the athletics department a chance to get to know each other as human beings with issues, values and significant others. I always had a lot of fun, even when Jeff announced sheepishly one evening that his son's pet snake had escaped and was missing.

As I recall, the party continued but everybody was alert. Very alert.

When Coach Staak left Xavier to take the head coaching job at Wake Forest, it was up to Jeff to find a coach to continue the momentum. I have always been grateful that he hired Pete Gillen. At the University of Notre Dame for several years as an assistant, he brought with him a strong tradition of academic excellence for athletes.

The timing was perfect.

The National Collegiate Athletic Association (NCAA) was waking up to its responsibilities, the university had made an official commitment to student athletes and along came Pete Gillen, who gave me an incredible tool. The benching privilege. It only made sense to me. "You bench a player when he misses practice," I said to him. "I want to bench a player when he misses class. Your players have to believe their education is as important as the game."

"Okay," he said. "Bark is no good without bite."

Word got around. If Sister says you're out, you're out.

Pete said at the beginning, "Working with these inner-city kids was new to her. She got duped a few times and so did I, but you can't fool her too often. She's pretty street-smart for a religious lady." If I was talking to a student for several weeks straight, and he was missing class, not doing assignments, I would make sure Pete knew about it. He'd talk to the student and tell him that he was benched. "When Sister calls me, you can play again," he'd say.

It helped that the NCAA was getting stricter, making it clear that academics was not a whim. But I always felt that with guidance the student-athlete would find something deeper, something beyond just eligibility for the next game. Simply buffing up a grade to manipulate the system, play until the institution gets what it wants is wrong. We cannot tell freshmen to give everything they've got, beat the tar out of everybody on our schedule and then at the end of November drop all the classes with Fs because the NCAA says all you need is a 1.75 grade point average. That's hardly putting academics first.

Pete said it like this: "Use basketball to make your life better. Don't let basketball use you. Use it. Get your degree. You'll need it when the air goes out of the basketball."

Like most all the coaches I've worked with, he knew his power, how much impact he had on the young men. He was their life coach as well as their basketball coach.

*O*nce when the team was on the road, two or three players started kidding around, sliding lighted matches under their teammates' doors in the hotel. Every once in a while, they reminded us that they were, after all, kids. The fire alarm went off. So did the coach. Furious, he gave them a safety lecture, then turned up the heat until he got the names of those directly involved. Some of the players thought the coach was making too much of an innocent prank. They were sent to visit the Shriners Burns Hospital when they got back to Cincinnati.

Brian Grant, incredible on the court, a rocky start in the classroom.

A good, a very good man, Coach Gillen truly wanted the best for the students, not that he didn't push them and not that he wasn't a fierce

> "His blistering pre-game tirades were legendary, and after a game, he was so sweaty, he looked like he had just played in it himself."

competitor. His blistering pre-game tirades were legendary, and after a game, he was so sweaty, he looked like he had just played in it himself. He piled up a long list of successes at Xavier during his nine seasons, leading the Musketeers to post-season play in eight of those years, including seven NCAA berths (six straight from 1986-91) and a trip to the NIT Quarterfinals in 1994.

XU also boasted seven twenty-win seasons under Coach Gillen. His career winning percentage of .729 (202-75) at Xavier was among the best for NCAA Division I coaches. He was the 1986, 1988, 1990 and 1993 Midwest Collegiate Conference (MCC) Coach of the Year, the 1988 Basketball Times Mideast Coach of the Year, and the 1989-90 Ohio Coach of the Year.

Impressive, to be sure. But I loved what he told his team many times. "We want to win, but we want to do it the right way."

As Xavier moved up from the Midwestern Athletic Conference to the more competitive Atlantic 10, recruiting became more aggressive. In some cases, our coaches were literally scouting pick-up games on blacktop courts in parks and neighborhoods, picking off the best shooters.

Coach Gillen often asked me to meet a potential recruit and his parents. "See if this guy can make it," he would tell me. Coaches promised recruits that Sister Rose Ann Fleming would help them through school. To some, that meant I "took care of things." They assumed they would not have to do anything except check in with me periodically and I would somehow magically get them through their classes. Basketball was the main event. Education was a by-product. Optional.

That's what happened with Brian Grant, who started playing basketball late in high school and surprised even himself when he turned out to be so good. When Coach Gillen finally saw him play during his final year of high school, he offered his last scholarship that season to the unknown from Georgetown, Ohio. He was one of my students in our summer Academic Bridge Program, intended to give incoming freshmen a leg up before they had to deal with the dual pressures of basketball and academics in the fall.

"Ms. Fleming, I really have to see you quick," he said one day after class.

I brought him downstairs to my office. He was scared to death. "Are these real classes I'm taking?" he said. "Real college courses?"

I said yes. Real classes. Real teachers. You'll earn seven real college credits—three in mathematics, three in English composition and one in critical reading. What's wrong?

He said he was under the impression that the Bridge Program was a bridge to basketball—a two-hour daily conditioning program in the weight room, practice games every night with older team members and pick-up games with some professional athletes who practice in the university field house. Oh, and some classes. He said, "I never dreamed this class stuff was going to count on our college record," he said. "I thought I was going to come work with the coaches and brush up my basketball skills and kinda' get ready for the fall."

> You are a very intelligent young man, and now that I have you in my clutches you are going to discover the wonderful world of books.

I explained that we take the "class stuff" seriously here. "We go to school and what we're doing now is helping you to get seven credits toward graduation before school starts. Besides that, you're getting to know the classes, the layout of the campus." I was giving him my sales pitch.

"I can't go on," he said. "I haven't done any work, and now we have midterms."

"You are not going to quit," I told him. "What do you mean you didn't do any work?"

"I haven't done the assignments."

"Well, Brian you've got to get them done," I said. " Let's talk to your teachers. You were invited in here late. You didn't understand fully what the program was about." And, p.s., although I didn't say it out loud, you are a very intelligent young man, and now that I have you in my clutches you are going to discover the wonderful world of books.

Brian and I sat down with the two other teachers and worked out a study schedule. He was definitely not afraid of hard work. Almost anything we asked him to do that summer was probably easier than what he usually did—picking and stripping tobacco, digging potatoes and baling hay. The physical labor made him strong, but it also made him determined to find something else to do with the rest of his life.

He caught up quickly and, by the end of the term, had passing grades. He went on to become a two-time Midwestern Collegiate Conference Player of the Year and honorable mention Associated Press All-American. He was inducted into the Xavier

Athletics Hall of Fame in 1999 and became one of only four players to have his jersey retired by the university. In his twelve years in the NBA, he played for five teams—Sacramento, Portland, Miami, Los Angeles and Phoenix—retiring in 2006.

All along the way, he was, as Richie Harris would say, putting cookies in the jar. Actually, he was cramming lots of cookies in the jar.

A Parkinson's disease fundraiser, where Brian puts more cookies in the jar.

Writing for *Xavier* magazine in the Fall of 2013, editor Skip Tate revealed an astonishing trail of good works, quietly performed by Brian Grant out of range of the media spotlight. When he was playing ball in Portland, a family named Thomas asked him to visit their 7-year-old son, Dash, who had brain cancer. They lived in Salem, Oregon, about an hour's drive from Portland. "Grant was so taken by the boy," Skip writes, "he wrote 'Dash' on his shoes before each game and drove back and forth to shoot baskets and play video games with the boy." The hour-long drives and visits continued for eight months until Dash Thomas died.

> **His generosity of spirit threaded its way through NBA cities where he played.**

After that, Brian started making regular visits to desperately sick kids at the Children's Hospital in Portland. "You see those families in there, and they have this look of, 'Help me I don't know what to do for my child.' That's who probably got the most out of it because they got to see their kid smile and laugh," he told Skip. "It was just a moment of peace, a moment they got to forget their child is dying. That's why I loved it too."

I believe, like so many of the young athletes I would meet, Brian had a hero's heart.

His generosity of spirit threaded its way through NBA cities where he played. He paid for the funeral of a murdered child. He organized a bone marrow drive. He encouraged school attendance with gifts of Blazer tickets. He befriended a young girl with leukemia, and helped raise the money for a $15,000 wheelchair van. He organized paintball outings for a grieving boy. He bought food and delivered it to the local Ronald McDonald House. Brian and his wife, Gina, provided Thanksgiving dinners for families in the Mothers Against Gang Violence program. At Christmas, they adopted families, showering them with presents—and time.

I visited Brian when he was with the Miami Heat. He had a beautiful Louisiana style home in Coral Gables. We went out to dinner and talked until late in the evening, a really nice opportunity to catch up with this exceptional man. A year or so later he signed with the Lakers in California. I called him and said, "Oh, no, you'll have to move from your beautiful home."

He said to me, "Sister, I am going where God wants me. I accept the change in that light."

In 2008, Brian was diagnosed with Parkinson's Disease, a neurological disorder that will slowly rob him of his amazing physical gifts. So, he began putting more cookies in a new jar. Using his fame and personality, he has raised more than $1 million for research and education. I have spoken to Brian since he was diagnosed, and, of course, I pray for him and think often of him and of the coach who brought him to me.

Pete Gillen trusted me and honored the work I do. He surprised me at the end of the 1991 season, when he named me Most Valuable Player. I will never forget his passion for the game, his concern for his players and his flair for the English language. "Please don't give him a nervous breakdown," he admonished once when he thought I should get off somebody's back. We didn't mince words with each other. And I will be forever grateful for these:

"Bark is no good without bite."

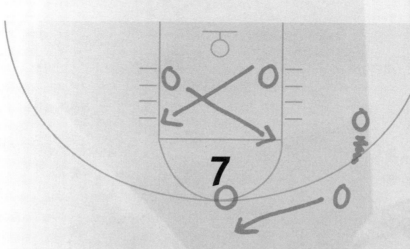

7

Scholarship is a Team Sport

The endgame with Stanley Burrell, Josh Duncan, and Father Mike Graham.

*P*layers who come to the study table are campus big shots. The other students know them, and they usually have been high school stars as well. Life's troublesome details often are handled by somebody else. If they wake up sick, their first instinct is to call the athletics trainer. Some have never had to make an airline reservation or a dental appointment. A team manager takes care of their clothes, hands them water and fetches balls. Somebody plans their meals and their housing. I've joked that sometimes these exceptional athletes lack the small motor skill to pick up a pencil and write something down.

As academic adviser, I knew I had to work with the "other team" that surrounds our players—coaches, faculty and administration—to get these young men to pick up the pencil, to follow directions from professors, to read, to be ready to assume control of a future beyond basketball. I began by studying the most important person in their lives, their coach.

We educators often say everyone doesn't learn the same way, but we rarely offer a choice beyond books and lectures.

Coaches are master teachers, resourceful and innovative, and I learned by watching them. They use videos. They praise. They exhort. They explain. They break complicated plays down into smaller parts. They scribble on white boards. They explain again. And again. They have players repeat things. Get up, walk around. They use all available media and interactive drills. They tell them. They show them. If you multiply that by history and English and theology and fine arts and math you begin to realize how much effort it takes to duplicate academically what is done for them on the court.

When a coach said, "See Sister," they did. Then it was up to me to play my part on their team, try to figure out what would work for them in the classroom. I was lucky to start my job as academic athletics adviser with Coach Pete Gillen as my ally. Granting me the benching privilege was huge, never mind that I used it only twice during our time together. I could if I needed to, and players knew it. That was usually enough. The nine-year tradition Coach Gillen started was extended by his successors.

Skip Prosser, who had been an assistant to Coach Gillen, set up a tripod in the locker room with a game plan for his first year as head coach. At the top was: "Academics First," which set the tone immediately. His favorite quote was from Ralph Waldo Emerson: "Our chief want in life is someone who will make us do what we can." Coach Prosser said he thought that was a powerful statement, that we need to be around people who challenge us to be as good as we can be. He made it clear that a player's best extended beyond athletics.

Our next head coach, Thad Matta, who came to Xavier from Butler University, often referred to "The Xavier Way," his vision of the athlete's focus on perfection to detail in academics as well as sports. When one of the players fell below academic standards, I set up a conference with Coach Matta and the athlete. After hearing the problem, Coach locked eyes with the athlete and said, "You're better than this. I know you very well because I have recruited you for two years. And so I know you can and will correct the situation." And the correction happened —with a lot of help from the rest of us on the team. But the coach pushed him in our direction.

> "Competing with other top-notch schools while maintaining academic excellence adds pressure and visibility."

Sean Miller, coach from 2004 to 2009, often asked me to meet with recruits and their parents as competition heated up for talent. He and his assistants introduced me as "the point guard," which carried the message to pay attention to me if they wanted to play. "Whatever she says goes," he told players. He was a great motivator and showed tremendous respect for the academic program.

The first thing young recruits see when they walk into our current head coach's office is a picture of Jamel McLean, who led the Atlantic 10 Conference in offensive rebounding during his senior year. Instead of an action shot on the court, Coach Chris Mack chose a photo of Jamel in a cap and gown, smiling as he receives congratulations from XU president Father Michael J. Graham, S.J. "I like pictures and images to tell the story of Xavier," Coach Mack says. "I want families to know it's about the total development of their son and leaving with a degree."

Entrance into the newly formed Big East, the nation's only non-football, basketball-centered power conference, is going to be a very good time for us. All the Big East schools except Butler are Catholic, so it offers the opportunity for subtle preaching of values and service on and off the field. The new league already boasts one not-so-subtle record. All of the Big East schools have an NCAA graduation rate of at least 90 percent, with the exception of Butler, which is at 83 percent. Xavier's 97 percent graduation rate for all eighteen of our sports teams puts us at the top of the list.

Competing with other top-notch schools while maintaining academic excellence adds pressure and visibility. It's going to be a challenge, but I know we can handle it. We just have to be vigilant, stick to what we've learned. On the academic side of the player's life here at Xavier, there is no manager to carry his books, no one who will write his papers, no one who will take his tests. We have to make sure both our faculty and our players accept that.

We are being watched by a bigger audience, and we'll be surprised how much greater we can be. We have history and the experience of success on our side, and we have vigorous and consistent support at the top. Beginning with Jeff Fogelson and continuing with athletics directors Dawn Rogers, Mike Bobinski and now Greg Christopher, Xavier has had a remarkable chain of academic backing from athletics leaders. Hired in March of 2013, Greg says players are on the front porch of the institution, the face of Xavier. It's a good way to put it.

He says one of the reasons he was attracted to Xavier was its academic values and the institutional commitment to student-athletes. "Every sport is equally important when they go in for fundamental resources. When they walk in the training room or study hall, it doesn't matter whether they are a basketball player or a swimmer. Help is available for anybody."

Tutors, who often meet with their students during study hall, range from retired faculty members from Xavier and other universities in the Cincinnati area to other students who have been hired and trained to work with our players. They all must qualify by learning both NCAA and Xavier rules. When I brought in adult tutors to "re-teach" the material or when I asked students to go over notes, I always made sure they had the appropriate training. The inviolate rule is that no tutor is permitted to do the work for the player. Their job is only to show the athlete how to learn the required material. This is not as easy as it sounds, and help sometimes comes from unexpected places.

An exceptional tutor came out of the courtroom to help Stan Kimbrough. A top player on Xavier teams in the late 1980s who went on to play two seasons in the NBA, Stan transferred here as a freshman from Central Florida University. "I grew up in the projects in Cleveland with a single mom. I was five feet, ten inches tall and weighed 135 pounds, soaking wet. "You might say I had a lot of determination."

A likeable guy, Stan was eager to get up to speed at Xavier, which he said was much harder than his previous school. He decided to major in social work, which meant he had to finish a lengthy research paper. Stan chose to explore Title IX and its impact on collegiate sports for women. His topic was approved, and he began investigating with energy and enthusiasm. Then he got stalled.

He had done hours of research, but he couldn't get started on the writing. Most of us who have stared at a blank piece of paper or, these days, a blank screen, can sympathize. Sports columnist Red Smith has been widely credited with the old saw: "There's nothing to writing. All you do is sit down at a typewriter and open a vein."

Yikes. We needed help, and it came from an attorney who had given me his card, maybe only as a polite gesture. Too bad for him. I am ruthless when it comes to a struggling student, and I knew that this lawyer had some experience with Title IX. His customary fee was $150 an hour, about ten times our going rate for tutors. For the better part of a semester, Stan and this attorney met almost every evening. Part mentor, part tutor, he taught Stan how to release what was in his head onto paper, and we never got a bill.

"You wonder when you start a new school if they'll throw you into classes just to keep you eligible,"Stan says. "It didn't take me long to see that wasn't the way it was going to work at Xavier. I was encouraged to take classes that would actually help me, that were hard but with stuff I could use." He says summer school before his senior year included a group dynamics class and a gospel story class.

"To this day, I use what I learned in those classes," he says. "The Biblical stories really clicked with me. I began to understand how a book can talk to you." The group dynamics class and some volunteer work he did that summer, he says, pointed him toward his life's work.

While he was a student, Stan interned as a counselor at St. Aloysius Orphanage in Bond Hill, a Cincinnati neighborhood northeast of downtown. He came back with stories of what they called the Sitting Chair. It was like being benched, he explained, but it was not a punishment. It was an enforced break so kids could watch how other kids were doing the work and how they behaved.

"Sister," he told me. "I could see how you could help children change, motivate them." He graduated with a degree in social work, then played for the Detroit Pistons and the Sacramento Kings before starting Kimbrough for Kids, an organization that teaches basketball fundamentals. He also volunteers as a reading and writing tutor.

That's key, as important as anything we do for these young people. I often think of Xavier as a crucible through which an athlete enters as a freshman and leaves with the Ignatian and academic values that surround him during his time with us. All our athletes are required to participate in at least one service project each semester.

Stan still remembers a service project that was not on the syllabus. I had to go out of town for a week, and I asked him to feed my fish while I was gone. "I really sweated

Athletics Director Greg Christopher and the Hoff memos, a remarkable chain.

Stan Kimbrough, determination and a fish story.

this," Stan says. "There were three or four of them in the tank. And I was scared to death one of them was going to go belly up. I found myself hanging over that tank all the time, making sure they were still moving and right side up. Sounds silly, but it meant so much to me to be trusted."

Not silly. Not silly at all. I respected Stan, and it was a way for me to show him. Plus, I really didn't know what else to do with the fish.

Stan Kimbrough came from a part of Cleveland that was so tough someone stole his best present one Christmas—a basketball. Shortly after Sherwin Anderson came to Xavier, he was stunned by news from home that his best friend had been jailed for murder. Like Stan, Sherwin remembers feeling alone and without a clue about how to handle his new life in a baffling new place. "I arrived on campus with a boom box and some clothes," he says. "I didn't know you needed all that other stuff. I didn't know how to study or go to class."

After finding his room on campus, he was so exhausted he dropped onto the bare mattress and fell asleep. There he sprawled, rap music blaring, when his new roommate arrived from Mentor, Ohio, trailing startled parents. "We were from two different worlds," Sherwin says, "but we became friends right away. That was Xavier. I opened his eyes. He opened mine."

When he was 8 years old, Sherwin came to the United States from Guyana on the northern coast of South America. "I lived in the projects in Brooklyn with my mom and dad and three uncles." The uncles were in and out of jail. His mother and father worked two jobs. "The neighborhood was lousy with gangs. We were poor. Really poor. Coach Gillen came to our place. He knew how it was for me."

By the end of his freshman year, Sherwin was on probation. "I had no idea how to study and take notes. I did not have the basic skills." He was on the verge of losing his basketball eligibility. He was bright. And he was ready to change. We threw everything and everybody we had at him. I'd roust him out of bed at 5 a.m. to meet with his Spanish tutor, then haul him out of practice that afternoon to meet with another tutor.

"It was a very hard road for me," Sherwin says. "Now I have an appetite for education, and I feel like I missed out on a lot of what I could have had at Xavier." He graduated early, finished a master's degree program in sports administration in 1997 and after a year on the road with the Harlem Globetrotters, set himself up as owner of a training program for youngsters. Now a voracious reader—everything from the *Tibetan Book of the Dead* to an exploration of modern dance—he says I taught him why learning is important. And Bill Daily from Xavier's communications department taught him how to golf and gave him a set of clubs for graduation.

Mike Bobinski once said, "If you don't turn out people who are better off than when they came in here, you're not doing your job." Talking about a player who graduated in 2002, Mike said, "He came with a lack of trust in others—particularly adult figures. By the time he graduated, he totally changed. He had a great basketball career, but our greatest success is how he changed as a person. It would have been a hollow victory if he graduated but was the same person he was when he came here."

It is not magic. It is discipline and training and determination. It is routine and persistence. It is, if I may say, finding good people to do good work. Our goal is to win the student's commitment to learning. Once we do that, we do everything in our power to support that commitment.

Study hall is open from 7 to 9 p.m. Sunday through Thursday, open to all athletes and compulsory for first semester freshmen and those whose grades are below 3.0. These are active sessions. A proctor or tutor checks in designated athletes and reviews with them the targets for learning they discussed earlier with their advisers. The students agree with the specialists on a set of strategies to accomplish one or more learning targets during the period, and, after the two hours, the learning specialists and the player evaluate what has been accomplished. If it's not finished, they stay until it is.

The weekly academic meeting printout is a rainbow of color-coded classes with notes on upcoming assignments, tutorial sessions, grades and comments. The older players are our best salesmen for the Time Out that study hall provides in the daily life of the athlete. It pulls them mentally back into the student mode. It's Richie Harris's advice, which I never forgot: Take time to learn.

We surround the athlete's day with an opportunity to learn, and we make certain they have one schedule that contains both their academic and athletics requirements. In other words, we build academics into their routine.

We give academics weight in their sports-oriented world. In general, their mornings are packed with classes and with meetings with advisers for at-risk athletes. At these weekly meetings, the advisers break down the students' syllabus learning targets. It helps them to tackle the semester's work in smaller chunks, which is less daunting to freshly minted scholars. They have a clear picture of their short-term goals when they leave the adviser's office.

Our mentoring program includes about twenty faculty members who volunteer their time to meet with coaches and see what they can do to boost the academic attitudes of the players within each team. It's a different, but no less important assignment than tutoring. The teams have different cultures. The larger teams have three or four mentors that work with them. They are available for recruits who come on campus, and they've also helped faculty understand the unusual academic hazards for student athletes.

The only academic perk our athletes get is the ability to jump line when registering for classes. It just makes sense for us to help them avoid conflicts with practice or road trips. Even so, they miss a lot of class with travel. We have a list of classmates willing to e-mail them notes from classes they've missed because of their athletics obligations. As soon as possible after the road trip, the note-takers meet with the athletes to confer and review these notes.

In return, we do not expect unexcused absences. At all. Ever. They have to take responsibility for making up missed work, and we have a stiff penalty for missing unexcused tutor appointments. If it happens twice, they must pay for the appointment.

We get progress reports from faculty every three weeks, which gives us the chance to try to help with problems in the earliest stages. Progress reports are augmented by software. Our "Early Warning System" lets faculty warn us of problems electronically by the end of the third week of school. They can also send "Hot Button" messages on the Xavier Portal immediately after class on such issues as attendance or failure to hand in critical assignments.

Even with all this technology, sometimes just sitting down together and talking is still the best tool we have. Never skip a class, I tell the student-athletes. Never sleep in class. Both are insulting to the teacher, which would be very poor game strategy. I admonish them never to report to class without homework. If there's a problem, let your teacher know before the class begins. Also, I say, your teacher has a name. Be sure to use it. Never forget to thank everyone who supports you: fans, students, tutors, professors, your coaches. Gratitude is a signal of a noble heart and yours, I assure them, is a hero's heart. I have seen it time and again and can point to men like Brian Grant as examples.

Some athletes are uncomfortable or hesitant about meeting with faculty. To some, the idea that their teacher is an actual human being is shocking information. It's one reason I think the mentor program for our teams is important. If they seem uneasy, I'll make appointments for them, then go with them to the conference.

Teamwork. It's the only way I've found to win our game—putting an athlete on the path to a degree. No matter how well-intentioned or committed we are, we have to be willing to reach out to a professor or tutor or a mentor or adviser who might be able to do something we can't. You have to work with others if you really want to help others.

Sometimes we have to pass the ball.

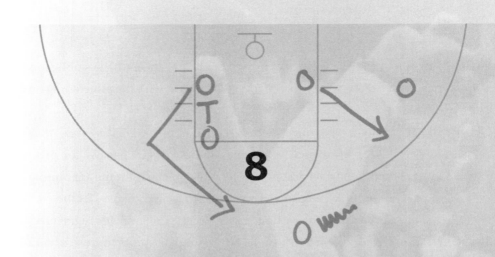

8

The Twin Towers: Tyrone and Derek

Tyrone Hill, a battle of wills off the court.

*I*t could have been a simple mistake or it might have been something more malevolent. The NCAA got an anonymous call saying high school basketball star Tyrone Hill wasn't qualified to get into college. Athletics director Jeff Fogelson asked me to see what I could find out.

Tyrone's high school, Withrow, is a beautiful brick complex on Cincinnati's east side, known for its arching entry bridge and 114-foot clock tower. George Clooney's Aunt Rosemary graduated from this school. So did Jimmy Dodd, head mouse of the original Disney Mouseketeers. But over the years, like most urban schools, Withrow has struggled. When I arrived on the campus in 1986 there were metal detectors at the front entrance.

Lionel H. Brown was principal. Dr. Brown, now on the faculty at the University of Cincinnati, was a tremendous asset to the school and an impressive presence. He has made urban students and their families a major focus for his scholarly research and life's work. Just then, he was giving this matter—and this particular urban student—his full attention.

Tyrone was the third youngest in a family of thirteen children. He likes to think of himself as the "baddest of the bad," Dr. Brown said. I do not think that Brown agreed with Tyrone's assessment. In fact, I think, in the words of my principal at The Summit, Sister Teresa Mary McCarthy, he thought Tyrone was interesting.

Then the educator looked at me across the desk—I'll never forget this—and said with conviction—"This young man deserves an opportunity for a college education." And neither of us was willing to have his future derailed by a spineless, anonymous phone caller. On my way to Dr. Brown's office, I had stopped off at the counseling office to pick up copies of Tyrone's records. I handed them across the desk, and after he inspected each one, he wrote a positive recommendation across the bottom of every page. We were free to recruit Tyrone, and he committed in April of 1986.

He came in that summer for the Academic Bridge Program. As is often the case, he thought the workouts and basketball scrimmages were the main event and classes were inconsequential. I broke the news to him about the scholastic work he had to do.

"I'm here to play basketball," he huffed.

"You are here to play basketball and to get an education," I huffed back.

That summer, we had study hall in the yellow-brick residence building called Kuhlman Hall, one of the oldest dormitories on campus. Updated, it was still decidedly modest. And hot. Tyrone was not pleased with the accommodations. We had resident tutor/counselors who were supposed to make sure Tyrone studied. He didn't like being told what to do. So he didn't. He also tried to persuade them to do his work. The counselors were cowed by him, but not so fearful that they didn't spill the beans to me when he didn't show up at the study table.

The next day, I would be in his face. Friendly, but firm, I would walk him through what was expected. It happened more than once. So when it came time for the confrontation over his philosophy paper, we knew each other. I already had a hunch that when I marched to the library he would follow. Years later, he would say, "If you could have, I know you would have picked me up and carried me over there. And I knew you were going to make me stay if it wasn't done right."

He respected me. And I respected him right back.

Besides his curiosity and intelligence, I genuinely admired his athletic ability, and I made it clear that I valued sports. I had several photos on my walls of Xavier teams and their coaches. I had just posted the 1987 basketball team's photograph. "Look at you, Tyrone," I said, "the tallest player on the team. I bet you make things happen at practice." And, naturally, I went to practice to see if I was right.

When he finished his philosophy paper, I persuaded him to have it professionally typed. I wanted him to know that academic work can be just as elegant as sinking a jump shot. And I wanted him to take pride in this ability, too.

So, we connected on respect and pride. And I still hadn't played the grandma card. I knew from Lionel Brown that although Tyrone may have had discipline problems growing up, he loved his grandmother and went to church with her when he was a boy. I heard later that during the summer before his senior year, he played pick-up games at a park in the city against Byron Larkin and that Byron had invited him to meet some of the Musketeers at Schmidt Field House. More good connections and good role models. More respect.

> I said if they promised not to crank up the volume on LL Cool J, I would try not to pray too loud.

Sometimes important bonds are formed just by being there. I think living at Manor House on campus was a distinct advantage. My work included finding students who didn't want to be found. And I could run like a deer.

When it was first announced that several basketball players were going to move into some of the twenty units in the Manor House complex, Tyrone called to warn me.

"You may want to move," he said.

"Why would I want to move?" I answered. "I've been there a while."

"Because we're moving in. It will be noisy."

The team had regular drug and alcohol testing, and they were typically exhausted during the season. They were not going to be up all night partying. I assumed the big reason they wanted me out of the way was because they thought I would complain about their music, which was sometimes earsplitting. I said if they promised not to crank up the volume on LL Cool J, I would try not to pray too loud.

One day, Tyrone came by and asked me to go see his grandmother in the hospital. I found the whole family gathered around her in the emergency room area. We joined hands in prayer. When she died a few months later, Coach Gillen and his entire team went to the funeral at the church. I, too, was honored to be among the mourners. Tyrone was completely torn up, hunched over with his forehead on his knees. His loss was anguishing. I admired him. I respected him. And I loved him.

Tyrone Hill was chosen by the Golden State Warriors in the NBA draft of 1990 and went on to play for Cleveland, Milwaukee and Philadelphia. Particularly while he lived on the West Coast, he called me every few weeks just to talk. "Sister," he said once, "I never wanted to disappoint you." And I never wanted to disappoint him.

For whatever reason—call it the Sister Anna Regis broom effect, Tyrone and I seemed to connect almost immediately. One of his closest teammates was a different story, one that by now is probably apocryphal, involving 129 rings of a phone.

Derek Strong played alongside Tyrone Hill for three years and will be forever linked to him in Xavier sports archives because of their nickname, the Twin Towers. Recruited from Watts, one of the poorest sections of Los Angeles, Derek was what's known as a partial qualifier, meaning he had to prove himself as a student before he could play basketball. Xavier was taking a chance on Derek. And vice versa. The Jesuit university in Cincinnati, Ohio, was a long way from his comfort zone and from his family.

When I finally got him to confide in me, he spoke of a sister who was close to him in age, and he had a grandfather whom he adored, "the only father I've ever known." His mother worked as a nurse's aide, and he went to school and came home by himself. When he could borrow one from his uncle, he'd race go-karts around the empty parking lots near his home. I don't think there was any way his mother could make sure he did his homework, and he just squeaked by in school.

Plucked out of Los Angeles, Derek was physically and emotionally isolated in Cincinnati for the first time in his life. Never an outgoing person, he became even quieter and more withdrawn. Toward the end of the first semester of his sophomore year, he suddenly stopped going to class. He had his schedule. He had his books. He just wasn't going to class, and finals were getting closer. The coaches were stumped, told me they were worried.

In those days, there was no e-mail and no cell phones. Very few people had answering machines on their land-line phones. I kept bugging the coaches to see if they'd figured out what was wrong with Derek. One morning, they told me Derek was definitely inside his apartment because they had just dropped off something for him to eat. So I called. No answer. I let it ring. I let it ring sixty-four times. Still no answer. I tried to imagine what Derek must be thinking. Did he know it was I? Who else would be so relentless?

I hung up. Gave up. Sat in my little office in Alter Hall a minute or two. Then changed my mind. I dialed again. It rang sixty-five more times. Then he picked it up. "You were driving him crazy," Coach Gillen told me later. This became known as the story of the 129 phone rings. And it was my foot in the door with Derek.

He began talking to me. I think I just wore him down. Like Donnie. Like Tyrone Hill, like most of us, he was afraid of failure. He didn't feel up to speed academically and was scared of flunking out. The more he studied, the more he realized he didn't know. The prospect of years of this was mortifying and depressing. And he didn't know how to ask for help.

As usual, once I believed I had an inkling of the problem, I forged ahead. Cheerfully but forcefully. Sort of like marching off to the library with Tyrone in tow. I began bringing in tutors and watched Derek's classes more carefully, sometimes sitting in on them. I spoke to his teachers, and together we really zeroed in on what was holding him up. He would tell me that he didn't want to go to a class because he did not understand something and couldn't ask the professor for help. Maybe he was afraid the other students would think he was stupid or maybe he was just mistrustful.

A hero's heart, I would remind him. You have a hero's heart. The university is proud to have you as its representative. Professors and your classmates feel privleged to help, I would tell him. And I meant it.

The Twin Towers: Tyrone and Derek

Tyrone Hill, Jamal Walker, Derek Strong and the legend of the 129 rings.

"If you can't ask the teacher, ask me," I told him. He did. Maybe the 129 rings told him something about my commitment to him. Maybe he just couldn't stand the thought of 129 more. Anyway, he rallied, worked hard and got through his final exams. I really pulled out all the stops trying to get Derek to talk to me, to trust me. And he did after what I suppose is the conversational equivalent of shamelessly persistent phone calls.

Later that year, Derek's mother called to tell him that his grandfather was ailing, the beginning of a terrible roller coaster ride for the family. The elderly man would rally, then be back in the hospital. One afternoon, I got a call from a secretary in the athletics department. Derek's grandfather had passed away, and nobody could find him to let him know. I tracked him down at the student center and asked him to come back to my office, where I broke the news to him as gently as I could.

His sobs sounded as if they were coming from his toes. I passed him a box of tissues and waited. Finally, he was ready to talk. I reminded him that he was surrounded by people who cared about him.

"Do you want a service here for your grandfather?"

"No."

"Would you like me to find a pastor from your church?"

"No. What I would like to do is to go to Bellarmine Chapel. I want you to come with me."

I stood at the door of the chapel, while Derek knelt in front of the lighted statue of Our Lady. I could see his lips moving but couldn't hear what he was saying. This seemed miraculous to me, and I hoped it would give him some peace. After a long while he stood up and asked about the nearby vigil candles.

In the Catholic Church, lighting a candle is a way of extending one's prayer and further honoring the person on whose behalf the prayer is offered. A donation is customary so the church can buy more candles. Some candles are small and cost maybe a quarter. The ones in Bellarmine are tall and really nice—dollar ones—and I didn't know if Derek had the money with him. Would I violate NCAA rules if I gave him money? You never know what might come back to haunt a player. So I just handed him the lighter. Someday, when I am not governed by basketball rules, I will go back and make it right with Bellarmine. I felt sure God and the pastor at Bellarmine and just about everybody else, with the possible exception of an anonymous caller to the NCAA, would forgive me.

Derek went on to become half of our Twin Towers. Six-foot-nine and six-foot-eight, respectively, Tyrone Hill and Derek lived up to their sports page nicknames. Besides being tall, they seemed to be able to pass the ball back and forth to each other, over the heads of opponents. Both were strong, physical players, not afraid to make body contact. We had a glorious run and showcasing the Twin Towers helped us recruit other talented players.

Inevitably, they attracted attention from the NBA. In Tyrone's junior year, he grappled with the choice presented to many top college players—should he accept offers to play pro ball or should he stay in college one more year and get his degree? The NBA offers big money, lots of attention, and the contract doesn't come with a bookbag and a nag. He asked me what he should do. In my head, I was shrieking, "Don't go. Don't squander your hard work. Don't. Don't. Don't." But part of what we try to teach our students is to become good stewards of their own lives, to make their own good choices.

So, I said calmly: "Tyrone, life is like strategy for a big game. If you maximize all the opportunities and minimize all the obstacles, you win." He decided to stay and collect the degree he had earned. So did Derek.

After graduating from Xavier in 1990 with a degree in communications, Derek Strong went on to play twelve seasons in the NBA. Since retiring from pro basketball in 2003, he has returned to the joy of his childhood. Instead of go-karts and makeshift parking lot race tracks, he became a professional stock car driver and owner of Strong Racing Team. He travels around the country, getting "seat time," competing with a fair amount of success, finishing in the top ten in more than two-thirds of his races. He's hoping to race in the Automobile Racing Club of America or the Camping World Truck Series, both minor league affiliates of NASCAR.

Sharing the education he got at Xavier, he has teamed up with the Memphis-based Motorsports Institute to help promote racing and reading. The Institute brings Derek and his cars to schools, but he wants them to see him race. The economic downturn cost him some key corporate sponsorships, so Derek is trying to line up sponsors. He's knocking on doors and working the phones. I believe the communications degree he earned at Xavier will be useful, and I like to think he might be inspired by the memory of the relentless little nun who knocked on his door and let his phone ring until she got the answer she needed.

The other half of the Twin Towers, Tyrone, retired from basketball after coaching for the Atlanta Hawks. My former neighbor spent time in Cincinnati, rebuilding a playground in the Evanston area where he grew up. For a while, he owned a company called All Net Records, which released various singles and albums by groups including OTR Clique, D'Meka, Renaizzance and KompoZur. I am not familiar with these artists, but I assume they are loud.

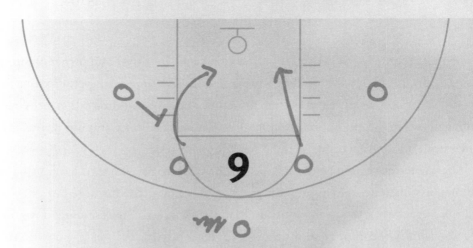

9

The Hoff Plan Moves Forward

Father Hoff put his beloved basketball to work for the university.

*T*wo memories of Jim Hoff are, to me, windows on the grand diversity of skills that shaped a modern Xavier University.

The first one, not surprisingly, happened on a basketball court. Father James E. Hoff, S.J., was in his customary floor seat at practice, although he was desperately ill. In January and February of 2004, the team, led by Coach Thad Matta, had been on a losing streak. When they took a break, Jim got up and limped over to the huddle. "Fellas," he said firmly, "this has got to stop." And we went to the Elite Eight that year, just a few months before Jim died.

Of course, Jim didn't make it happen. Of course not. But he surely was an extreme fan and he had faith. He not only went to all the games, but he went to many of the practices. At a practice years earlier, Coach Skip Prosser asked Father Hoff if he had any words for the team. He did. "Boys, if you rebound more than they do, if you turn the ball over less than they do, if you score more points than they do, there's a good chance we will win."

Case closed.

The second memory, I think, defines his demanding leadership and tough standards. Doris Jackson and I had started an Honors Day, recognizing the academic achievements of our athletes. Three deans attended, plus the athletes and, to our delight, the president of the university. The next day Father Hoff called me into his office to congratulate me, to tell me how much he enjoyed the ceremony. He had a coach's clipboard with some sheets of yellow legal paper attached. He handed me the papers, on which were handwritten notes—twenty-five ways to improve Honors Day before the next one. And this was a program he liked. Imagine the instructions attached to projects he didn't like.

As President of Xavier from March 1991 to December 2000, he directed monumental physical and academic changes, never losing sight of the school's mission: "to prepare students intellectually, spiritually and morally to take their place in a rapidly changing global society and to work for the betterment of that society."

Up to this point, Xavier presidents were coming and going at an unseemly fast pace. Charlie Currie left for Georgetown after four years. Four years later his successor, Father Albert DiUlio left to head up Marquette. Midland Company executive and Xavier trustee Michael Conaton took the reins temporarily while a search was mounted. When Father Hoff accepted the job, he told the crowd assembled in Music Hall at his installation that he would stay for at least ten years. Everybody clapped.

They'd have clapped and turned cartwheels if they'd known how good he would be.

Before he came to Cincinnati, he taught theology and ethics, coached high school basketball, directed a medical school, raised money, counseled terminally ill patients and trained Jesuit novices. He came from Creighton University, where he was vice president of university relations and president of the Creighton Foundation. Before that, he nearly became a physician. He was accepted to the Marquette University School of Medicine in 1963, but entered the Society of Jesus instead and was ordained in 1965. A year later, he earned a master's degree in theology from St. Louis University and his doctorate in theology from the Gregorian University in Rome in 1969.

> **Father Hoff firmly and purposefully anchored the nomadic men's basketball team to campus.**

Of course, nobody ever called him Dr. Hoff. I tried calling him Father Hoff, but early in our relationship, he said, "I'm not your father. Call me Jim." So I did. I was enormously fond of him and respected him a great deal. He loved sports, but not as much as he revered education. His genius would be to use athletics as the engine, the force behind academics.

The classroom was to be a beneficiary of the arena, not a casualty. When Father Hoff arrived at Xavier the average incoming freshman's GPA was 2.9. It was 3.46 when he retired. The average SAT scores for freshmen rose more than 150 points. He created the university's first doctoral program, in psychology and the weekend degree program for adult students.

He had a plan.

First was growth, bricks and mortar growth. As I walked around campus during his years with us, I could see his hand everywhere. As I had been in my early years at The Summit and at Trinity College, he was counseled by a members of a diverse and active board of trustees, who worked with him to "fill the factory." He filled it, then enlarged it, then filled it some more.

A new dorm, Buenger Hall, opened on campus in 1994 with suites for more than 200 freshmen and sophomore athletes and honors students. Jim knew that what a student learned at our institution was most important, but they had to choose to come here first. They—and their parents—had to like the looks of the place. Brick walkways and green spaces bloomed from the dorms through the center of campus by 1996.

He closed a large portion of Herald Avenue, turning it into a grassy mall. A stretch of Ledgewood Drive that split the heart of the campus also was closed to automobile traffic, making it safer for our students walking to class, and prettier too.

The university didn't just get bigger, it got bigger thoughtfully, with grace and taste.

Xavier's castle architecture with its turrets and picturesque stance on Victory Parkway was preserved, but more than $3 million was poured inside the old buildings. Schmidt, Edgecliff, Schott and Hinkle halls were refurbished, and construction begun on the Gallagher Student Center and The Commons apartment complex. Big. Important. But the Cintas Center was the cornerstone of his plan. The five-level building with its arena, student dining area and conference center is less than 200 yards from Xavier's residence halls. Calling Cintas Center the campus "living room," Father Hoff firmly and purposefully anchored the nomadic men's basketball team to campus.

For all this, he needed serious money. Once he explained the need, he assumed people would get on board. "Here's our plan," he would say. "What part of it appeals to you?" Everybody knew he wasn't seeking anything for himself. People loved him, trusted him and they did get on board. He could inspire and turn up the heat at the same time. Somebody asked Jim what he wanted for Xavier University, and he answered blithely: Everything.

The Century Campaign during his tenure raised $125 million, and Xavier's endowment soared from $24 million to $86 million. Meanwhile, he organized alumni into a national association, now with fifty chapters. They bring money, loyalty and, best of all, their children to the school.

Greg Christopher, Xavier's director of athletics, says when he was considering the idea of coming here from Bowling Green State University, he was swayed by Father Hoff's archived memos. "He looked way down the road. His plan worked. There's no better story of growth in the country than Xavier over the last three decades."

Basketball has put Xavier in the national spotlight, accounting for about half our media coverage. "Our society gives more attention to certain sports. Basketball has more wrapping paper. We averaged 10,000 people watching our basketball games," Greg says. "Basketball is the flagship. It's probably the most visible thing Xavier does. Not the most important thing, but the most visible thing."

Father Jim Hoff's vision was to put basketball to work for the rest of the university. Use basketball to get attention. Use the attention to get students. Let athletics hold the door open for admissions. Then we can teach them. "Faith is important to me.

Education is important to me," Greg Christopher says, "and I was drawn to a place where the values are mine."

In 2013, for the first time in Xavier history, more than 50 percent of freshmen came from out of state. "The Big East platform." Greg says, "is very intentional for university growth and consistent with Father Hoff's original plan. Xavier has gone from a good local institution to a regional institution and needs to become a national institution. We play basketball in markets where we need to attract students in order to grow."

When Xavier plays in a Big East city, on game day the staff hosts a reception for alumni and friends: Philadelphia, Chicago, Omaha, Indianapolis, Milwaukee, Providence, New York City, Newark and Washington, D.C. The crowds usually number between 200 and 300. Father Michael J. Graham, who succeeded Father Hoff, seizes these opportunities to tell Xavier's story in his unique style, with his deep voice resonant and his manner at once welcoming and authoritative.

"Xavier has a good basketball team, and it educates its athletes," he says. "Without the second part, the first part is not a story."

When Father Hoff announced he was stepping down in 2000, no one was surprised when his executive assistant moved into the president's office. Father Graham was immediately a reassuring and highly regarded presence, familiar in boardrooms, chapels and classrooms. He first came here in 1984 as an assistant professor of history after earning a Ph.D in American studies from the University of Michigan in 1983. He left to pursue his master of divinity degree in 1988 from The Weston School of Theology. Before that, he'd earned degrees in philosophy and psychology. He entered the Society of Jesus in 1978 and was ordained a priest in 1988.

In 1989, he returned to Xavier for good. And I mean that in a very literal sense.

Mike was appointed the vice president for university relations in 1994 and the executive assistant to the President in 1999. He led the ambitious fund raising during the Hoff years. The capital campaign during his own tenure raised more than $200 million with another campaign, now in the "quiet phase," expected to raise another $24 million.

Bearded, bespectacled, indefatigable, he lives on campus and remains an active parish priest at both Good Shepherd Catholic Church in suburban Cincinnati and at Bellermine with Xavier student groups, celebrating weddings, baptisms and retreats.

His 10 p.m. Sunday Mass is one of the most popular student gatherings on campus. "My model is Al Bischoff," he says, naming a beloved Jesuit priest, known throughout the campus as Father B.

"I'm a priest and I'm a teacher," he says. "My gifts and experience intersect with Xavier University at this moment in time in such a way that I think I'll be able to contribute an enhanced sense of the university's excellence as a university, per se, and as a distinctly Jesuit-Catholic university."

He, too, has a plan.

Fulfilling his vision of the "University as Citizen," Father Graham initiated the Community Building Collaborative and established the Eigel Center for Community-Engaged Learning, activities that connect the university to surrounding neighborhoods and the larger community. The Edward B. Brueggeman Center for Dialogue, established in 2002, positioned Xavier as a place for inter-religious activities.

"My signal achievement as president," he says, "is community engagement."

Quick to recognize and credit others, he led posthumous tributes to Father Hoff, retiring a basketball jersey in his honor, and commissioning a sculpture of him. In March of 2013, announcing the move to the Big East, he publicly thanked and praised longtime Athletics Director Mike Bobinski who was leaving Xavier for Georgia Tech that day.

In 2010, Mike dedicated the James E. Hoff, S.J. Academic Quad, which includes the Stephen and Dolores Smith Hall, a new home for Williams College of Business.

Father Mike Graham driving the mission forward, reaching out to the community.

Inside this technology-rich building is the Fifth Third Training Center with more than forty Bloomberg terminals and a trading room for analysis of stocks and securities and portfolio management. The quad also houses the Michael J. Conaton Learning Commons, a high-tech facility for career development, and the Sedler Center for Entrepreneurship and Innovation, teaching students to recognize and seize business opportunities. The Institute for Business Ethics helps students bring spiritual and moral values with them into the workplace.

In 2011, Xavier opened its second largest building on campus, Bishop Edward Fenwick Place. Set in the heart of campus, it is home to 535 students, can seat more than 700 at mealtime and offers large and small office spaces. Overseeing this development is an eleven-foot statue of the university's patron saint and one of the first Jesuits, Francis Xavier. His outstretched hand welcomes all.

Xavier University's neighbors have accepted the invitation.

The Port of Greater Cincinnati has earmarked money to redevelop portions of Evanston. There are about one hundred properties within the targeted area in Evanston between Dana Avenue and Madison Road near the campus for rehabilitation or new construction. University Station, an expansive new $54-million mixed-use development on fifteen acres abutting campus on the east includes an 11,000-square-foot Xavier University bookstore, a 180-unit apartment complex, 35,000 square feet of dining and retail space, 46,000 square feet of office space and every modern university's dream—more parking. About 1,000 spaces.

TriHealth was the first office tenant to sign a lease at the development, which faculty sees as new potential for internships for their students in health services and medical disciplines. TriHealth doctors, long-time health care providers for our sports teams and spectators at Cintas Center, will be more accessible, plus the system will bring new or expanded medical services to the rest of the neighborhood.

On the heels of the TriHealth announcement came word of another new medical neighbor. CTI Clinical Trial and Consulting Services, a drug development and research company, brought fifty new jobs and more educational opportunities. Former XU faculty member Dr. Candace Gunnarsson, a CTI executive, forecasts opportunities in recruiting future CTI employees, as well as the chance for partnerships and research.

Exactly. Sharing resources. Part of the Graham plan. "I try to take advantage of the opportunity that the world presents," Father Graham says simply. "And I'm a devoted listener."

Father Jim Hoff, who stayed on campus as chancellor working beyond his ten-year pledge with the development office and teaching theology, was diagnosed with cancer during the 2003-2004 Atlantic 10 basketball tournament. Xavier upset undefeated St. Joseph's in that tournament before going on to defeat Dayton for the A-10 championship and a trip to the NCAA Elite Eight. By then, he'd had surgery on both knees, as well as debilitating cancer treatments. I saw him literally crawl up the steps in hotels as we traveled to games. With a smile and steely determination, he always managed to make his way to his seat in Cintas Center, and he continued to say Mass on Mondays in Bellarmine Chapel.

"I was in Atlanta in March when I heard Jim had cancer," said Bob Kohlhepp, a Xavier trustee and one of Father Jim Hoff's closest friends. With access to a private plane, Bob said he offered to fly Father Hoff "anywhere, anywhere in the world." He asked to go to the Kohlhepps' place in Snow Mass, Colorado, just outside Aspen.

"I feel close to God there," Father Hoff said. He wanted to go in late May, although Bob warned him that the weather would be warmer later on. He didn't have time to wait, and I think he knew it, although doctors were giving him a year.

He died in July of 2004 at the age of 72 at his campus residence, surrounded by friends. To say they were friends and admirers would be redundant.

"He was my mentor, unselfishly sharing his wisdom and preparing me for my role to succeed him as president," Mike Graham said. "Jim raised the bar at Xavier and set a tone that pushed the University, and all of us associated with it, to dream big and strive to be better."

If Father Jim Hoff pivoted, Father Mike Graham drove us toward the net. He invigorated the mission, increasing the number of faculty, enhancing interdisciplinary study and expanding academic service learning and study abroad. He motivated faculty to update core curriculum and has reached out to the national and international community without loosening his embrace of friendship to Xavier's neighbors in Cincinnati.

As I live in the midst of a renaissance in Xavier's corner of the world, much of it the result of the patient, steady work of these two exceptional men, I am gladdened by my decision three decades ago to find my life's mission here, at this institution shaped and tended by the Society of Jesus. I also am gladdened to remain on the path set for my order by St. Julie Billiart to serve the disadvantaged through education. Defying the conventional wisdom at that time of a bleak and vengeful God, instead she told her followers: "How good is the good God! He is, He's around and He's good."

What a marvelous gift of leadership the good God chose to bestow on this place.

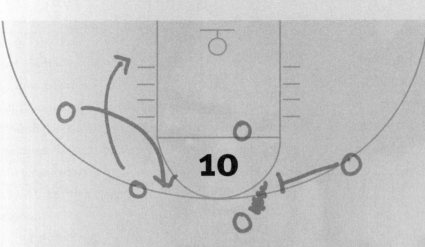

10

Skip Prosser Takes Over

When Pete Gillen left, Jeff Fogelson was
determined to bring Skip Prosser back to Xavier.

Not to rely too predictably on basketball metaphors, but I would say that Xavier, as a university, has bench strength. In administration, faculty and athletics.

Losing good leaders has been, of course, painful at times but has not weakened us as an institution. When Father Hoff stepped aside, Father Graham was ready. And when Pete Gillen left us for Providence College, a familiar and capable coach stepped in.

One of the first things I remember when Skip Prosser became head coach in 1994 was his phone call asking me to meet him for breakfast. When we sat down at the Frisch's in Norwood, I was curious and puzzled. I had known him for many years and admired and liked him. We'd worked together to help some struggling students. He was the assistant coach responsible for pushing Tyrone Hill my way at the beginning of my career at Xavier. Hired about the time I was named academic athletics adviser, he was Pete's top assistant for eight seasons before he left Xavier to take the head coaching job at Loyola in Baltimore.

Skip really liked Loyola, I think, and they must have loved him. Their basketball team had been losing for six seasons when he took over in 1993. He so completely turned them around that they went to NCAA post-season play during his first and only year there. When Pete left, Jeff Fogelson was determined to retrieve Skip Prosser for Xavier. I don't know if Jeff let Skip's phone ring 129 times, but I think he would have. He was absolutely convinced that Skip was the guy. And he was right.

The Musketeers went to six straight post-season tournaments during his seven years as head coach, and Coach Prosser accumulated an overall record of wins that was second only to Pete.

I like winning basketball games as much as the next rabid Musketeer fan, but it was the breakfast at Frisch's that, for me, revealed the genuinely winning nature of Skip Prosser. Making a point to sit down with me one-on-one before the season started was a clue to the value he placed on academics. He said he wanted to make sure I would stay with him as athletics adviser. I had no thoughts of leaving, and I suspect he knew that, but it was a mark of respect for our program that he didn't take it for granted. He followed up with that tripod on his first meeting with the players: Academics First. And it wasn't just window dressing.

If somebody was having a problem with his studies, I could always count on Skip to pitch in. Lenny Brown was a chronic challenge. Lenny said of himself more than once, "I'd be dead or still selling drugs if it wasn't for basketball."

A lot of Xavier fans still remember Lenny as the player who scored one of the most memorable baskets in Xavier history in 1996. We were playing our cross-town rivals, the University of Cincinnati, in their arena, Shoemaker Center. Called the Crosstown Shootout, this rivalry was fierce, and we were behind with just seconds left. Lenny got the ball and hit an off balance jumper, scoring in the final second. We won 71-69. Sportscaster Andy MacWilliams screamed, "UC is number one in the country and number two in their hometown. Xavier beat them on their own court."

The team celebrated noisily directly in front of UC Coach Bob Huggins and the Bearcats team bench. That was probably like gasoline on the flames of our already heated rivalry.

But that was a great night for Lenny, one of the best of his life he would say years later. Lenny almost gave up on school once, but was drawn back by charismatic coaches and his own courage. He was a terrific player, but I think he was playing for exactly the right man, a man who could bring out the best in him, a man who made him feel valuable. Skip liked Lenny, loved his toughness and, I think, understood him and was able to channel that aggression into basketball.

George Edward "Skip" Prosser could be tough, too. He grew up in Pittsburgh, where he played high school football and basketball and became a lifelong Steelers fan. He graduated from the U.S. Merchant Marine Academy and earned his master's from West Virginia University. My mental image of him at games is of his nimbus of red hair in disarray but with his silk necktie still tightly knotted.

After a losing game, I was with the team in the locker room. Skip was so angry he hit the concrete block wall with his hand, dislocating his little finger. His face was white and he must have been in enormous pain. He held out his hand to the team doctor, who pulled the finger back into place. Skip turned back to the team and finished his rant. He never used foul language, no matter how heated the harangue, but a barrage of frickin', frickin', frickin' in creative combinations was not uncommon.

Even tough exhortations were, somehow, elegant. "The greatest tribute you can give an opponent is to crush them," Coach Prosser told his team. "It shows you've prepared for them."

In those days, the basketball team still traveled on commercial airplanes, and Skip always insisted that they be dressed neatly and act like gentlemen. This was before Casual Fridays and when fancy restaurants like Cincinnati's Maisonette would refuse to seat men who were not wearing a coat and tie. So, when the team went to alumni gatherings, Coach Prosser told them to dress in a suit and "look these men right in the eye. They might have a job for you someday." Alvin Brown paid close attention.

Lenny Brown celebrating after the win against UC, gas on the flames.

He used to tell people that from the time he was a little boy he wanted a job where he could carry a briefcase.

Xavier alum Robb Schueler, who worked for Chrysler Finance as an auditor, found summer jobs at his company for Alvin and his teammate Maurice McAfee. Today, they probably carry laptops and iPads and Smartphones instead of briefcases, but the Xavier guards, best friends and roommates, made the most of their opportunity. Alvin has a job in Washington, D.C., in auto financing, and Moe McAfee is a project manager with U.S. Bank in Cincinnati.

"They were like our adopted kids—although they had wonderful families of their own," Martha Schueler says. But Moe's parents had to make a five-hour drive from their home in Saginaw, Michigan, to come to a game, and Alvin's folks lived in Washington, D.C. "We were proud to be stand-ins," Martha says. In the years before YouTube and endless internet caches, Martha was the informal Xavier basketball archivist, running out to buy multiple copies from Cincinnati's then-multiple newspapers, presenting graduating seniors with scrapbooks of their years with the team. She says she was surprised when NBA star David West, who plays now for the Indiana Pacers, approached her at a reception to tell her he'd just shared his scrapbook with his daughter. "Such a lovely man and so thoughtful to have remembered me," Martha says.

When Martha needed "the boys," they were there for her, too. Robert Schueler collapsed and died in 2005, and Alvin and Moe were at the funeral service. "It was always about more than just basketball," Martha says.

The Schuelers traveled with the team on a trip to Anchorage, Alaska. "People in the gift shop stopped us to tell us how polite, how nice these young men were. I credit Skip for

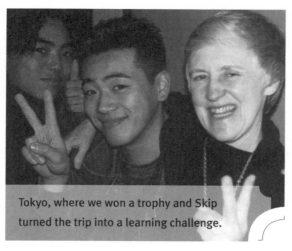

Tokyo, where we won a trophy and Skip turned the trip into a learning challenge.

a lot of that," she says. The players respected him, and he gave them clear boundaries and a huge dose of discipline. He also gave them a huge dose of religion, finding priests to say Mass when Xavier was on the road, and asking Father John LaRocca to offer Mass with the team at home before every game.

If the team was going overseas, Skip tried to find a course he could link to the trip, helping them eke a little more learning out of the experience. They went to England, Ireland and Wales. He encouraged the players to take a summer class in Irish history taught by Dr. Richard Gruber, professor emeritus, and he signed up for it himself, did all the reading, took the tests, wrote the papers. A very smart guy and a great reader. He loved to toss off quotes from Kant and Shakespeare and Nietzsche and Churchill.

When you talked to him it was not all hoops. He sponsored Dawn Rogers, Xavier's first female athletics director, when she converted to Catholicism. She told me he was helpful and encouraging. No surprise that a well-read fellow who could quote poets and philosophers could quote our Savior as well. He was a generous and complex human being. I was a charter member of his fan club, but the roster was packed. Nobody didn't like him. And we probably all liked him for different reasons.

My relationship with Skip worked so well, I think, because we both wanted the same thing for our student athletes. As Father Hoff would say: Everything.

Michael Perry, who was a sports reporter for the *Cincinnati Enquirer* during the Prosser years and whose book *Xavier Tales* is probably the most authentic and comprehensive history of men's basketball at the university, remembers Skip's basic fairness and his ubiquitous teaching moments. After a tough loss, one of our players refused to talk to a reporter. The day after the game, Skip dragged the athlete out of the locker room and shoved him at the reporter, saying, according to Michael, "If you can talk to her after we win, you can talk to her after we lose."

The *Enquirer* reporter had unfettered access to the team during Skip's years, including the pre-game talks. Michael remembers one in particular: "Everybody was kneeling. Skip told them to close their eyes and think of the person who meant the most to them, somebody who helped them get to the place where they were that day. 'Now, play this game for them,' Skip said."

Michael chuckles about practice sessions when "some big strong tough-minded athlete with swagger would walk in and lose the swagger when Coach said Sister wanted to talk to him. Right away."

A coach for his own fifth grader, Michael says he frequently finds himself repeating things he learned from Coach Prosser. "He used to say he wanted his players to be like a basketball, not a football. You can depend on the way a basketball will bounce, right back to you, consistent. A football is oddly shaped and will bounce all over the place. You never know what to expect."

Musketeers coach Chris Mack was a two-year captain when he played at Xavier for Pete Gillen and Skip Prosser. Skip was the one who brought Chris into the coaching ranks as Xavier's director of basketball operations before hiring him as an assistant at Wake Forest.

"Not a day goes by that I don't use some phrase or expression that Coach used. But it's a lot more than that," Coach Mack says. "Just being around Coach every single day, the way he carried himself, the way he treated people. He knew everybody's name in the athletics department. He knew everybody's name in the maintenance department. He was a genuine person."

Cintas Center had only been open for about a year when Wake Forest made Skip an offer he apparently couldn't refuse. I walked over to the athletics offices in 2001 after I heard, and they were empty. That's the way it would go. A coach would leave, and there was an immediate exodus of most assistants. No hard feelings. Just the business of sports. Skip, of course, kept in touch. That's the kind of man he was. He'd call me out of the blue when he was in the car traveling. "How are you doing? What's going on?"

Coach Thad Matta was Skip's replacement, and Thad told Michael Perry that Skip mentored him through his three years at Xavier. "A lot of times when a guy leaves somewhere, they probably want the next guy to fail. He was not that way." In *Xavier Tales*, Michael writes, "Though he was at Wake Forest, Prosser took the time to go through each returning player with Matta, telling him whatever he needed to know about the guys on and off the court."

Like everyone else who knew him, I was so sad and shocked when I heard the news of Skip's death in July of 2007. He was only 56 years old. He had come home from a punishing recruiting and meeting trip, hopscotching cities, hotels and plane flights. He flew home so he could speak at a Wake Forest basketball camp. He went for a run in the Carolina heat, then collapsed in his office and died of a heart attack.

"We had no warning," his widow, Nancy, says. "He was never sick, but coaching is a tremendously demanding job, physically and mentally. He thought about basketball when he went to bed at night, during the night and when he got up in the morning. And he really loved those kids."

They knew it. I think kids always know when they are loved. His players at Wake Forest tacked up posters at the school. "Skipisms," they called them, words they remembered from their coach:

"Playing time is not like Halloween. Just because you have a uniform doesn't mean you're going to get any candy."

"Never delay gratitude."

"The gym is the best place you'll ever be."

"Never, never give up."

"If you can't be on time, be early."

David West had the words "carpe diem" tattooed on the back of his calves, carpe on the left and diem on

> " From half a world away, soldiers in Kuwait posted anguished condolences on the internet. "

the right, a tribute to the coach who urged his team to "seize the day." A Wake Forest player with a mass of dreadlocks was teased by his coach, who wondered how many more free shots he could have practiced with the time he spent working on his hair. The young man cut his hair after Skip died.

From half a world away, soldiers in Kuwait posted anguished condolences on the internet. Just months earlier, Skip had traveled there to coach U.S. troops in a friendly but competitive week-long tournament.

"We just had a week, but he meant so much to us."

"The kind of guy you would want to have coaching your kid."

"Skip was a terrific person," Mike Bobinski said at the time of his death. "What I feel most sad about is that I know how much Skip looked forward to retirement with his wife, Nancy, and his family."

Nancy Prosser returned to Cincinnati after Skip's death and works as a nurse in the emergency room at University Hospital. "I still miss him every day."

His son, Scott, works in Pittsburgh and his other son, Mark, is an assistant basketball coach at Winthrop College in Rock Hill, South Carolina, working for head coach Pat Kelsey. More than 850 people gathered at Cintas Center for Skip's Xavier memorial service. Pat, who played for Skip at Xavier and was his assistant at Wake Forest, delivered the eulogy. "I don't know anyone who didn't like him. He was the best coach in basketball who didn't have an enemy."

My old friend and student Tyrone Hill, who was in the crowd that day, said he was surprised by the number of people who came to pay respects to his coach. "He was so personal with you. Sometimes you think you're the only one."

Coach Chris Mack said: "He was a better person than he was a coach. And he was a great coach."

11

The Road
Not Taken

Still in a starched shirt and tie, Richie
Harris took the road less traveled to head
up his own company.

About one percent of Division I college athletes are drafted into the NBA. Roughly 100 percent of Division I college athletes believe they might be in that one percent.

What happens if they stake their lives on it? What if the entire focus of a young man's four years at our university is basketball, and he is not invited to the NBA's legendary Green Room and a chance at a multimillion-dollar bid and the bonanza of selling his name to Nike and Reebok for millions more? And if he makes it into that storied one percent, there are no middle-aged men throwing elbows under the basket. Say he gets to play for ten years. What will he do with the next half century of his life?

The course on critical reading I have taught for thirty years includes Robert Frost's "The Road Not Taken," which the poet himself called "very tricky." The last stanza reads:

> I shall be telling this with a sigh
> Somewhere ages and ages hence:
> Two roads diverged in a wood, and I—
> I took the one less traveled by,
> And that has made all the difference.

Nearly all Xavier's basketball players have taken this class, and maybe I'm kidding myself but it seems to me they understand immediately the "tricky" part. That sigh. Was it one of relief? Or of regret? I think they are attracted by the poem's honesty and simplicity, and I know that many of them already had wrestled with difficult choices. And they would be faced with many more.

Eddie Johnson, one of Coach Staak's early recruits, comes to mind when I think about missed opportunities. Or, in Eddie's case, a near miss. A very big guy who was a high school standout in Baltimore, he was starting center for Xavier for two seasons, then was diagnosed with acute pancreatitis in September of 1983. He lost about fifty pounds, two months of school and a whole season of playing.

The next summer, he caught up on his studies and spent a lot of time in the gym and weight room. I really admired him, and I know his mother, Margaret Johnson, had a lot to do with his determination. He was back on the team again for the 1984–85 season, playing next to Richie Harris and Byron Larkin, who was a freshman that year. He played his senior year for Pete Gillen, then left school just nine credits short of a degree. He wanted to play pro ball and signed with a team in Europe, playing in Germany and South America for a couple of years, then enlisting in the U.S. Army.

In the locker room, the outrageous notion of a life after basketball.

When he telephoned in 1991, I could hear explosions in the background. He had been deployed to Saudi Arabia during Operation Desert Storm. "I'm okay, Sister," he told me, "It's just bombs. Not real near."

It sounded plenty near to me. We talked for about an hour. His tour of duty was almost up, and he wondered what his chances were to get back into school.

We'll figure it out, I told him. And we did.

He finished his liberal arts degree that same year. "Boy, I can still remember my mother's face when I walked across that stage to get my diploma," he says. A twenty-year veteran of the Baltimore Police Department, he still has his mother on speed dial.

"I liked that guy who recruited him—Coach Staak," Mrs. Johnson says. "We're Catholic, so I liked Xavier for that reason. I told him to go back, that they wouldn't give up on him."

Of course not. When our coaching staff goes after an athlete based on what he can do for us on the basketball court, the rest of us owe him a chance to collect on the bargain, to get something lasting at the end of his college basketball career. Even if it takes a while. And we owe him a chance for a bigger life—one that includes personal development beyond the classroom—a sense of purpose, exposure to the arts, camaraderie outside sports, the satisfaction of service to others.

My spiritual heritage began with those stouthearted nuns who bucked cruel traditions to bring education to the desperately poor and who traveled to Cincinnati to bring more than the three R's to students there, giving identical opportunity to the poor and to the wealthy to see planets revolve around the sun, to touch fine lace, to know the landscape beyond the cobbled streets of their city.

When a student-athlete comes to Xavier, if high school grades don't pass muster, we need evidence that he has the ability to catch up, that we are not asking something impossible for him to deliver. We are not alone in this. Since 1985, NCAA's Proposition 48 stipulates that an athlete has to qualify based on a sliding scale of test scores and GPAs.

In other words, if the recruit's grades are low, test scores have to be high. An athlete who has, for instance, a high school grade point average (GPA) of 3.0, needs only a 620 on his SAT test or a 52 ACT score. With a GPA of 2.5, the student must score at least 820 on the SAT or 68 on the ACT test. The intent is obviously to give athletes reasonably good odds for academic success. We often work with an athlete through our Summer Bridge Program to help him get a running start on his freshman year, but sometimes there's too much work to do in such a short time.

In 1998, Brandon McIntosh was a basketball and football star at Roger Bacon High School in St. Bernard, a small community just west of downtown Cincinnati. "Skip Prosser told me he was thinking of me for the basketball team," he says, "but my grades weren't good enough. My fault. Sometimes when you're young and immature, you don't see the big picture."

"Coach said he was sure I was intelligent enough to catch up. He said if I could prove myself academically after a year, he would help me play basketball. But he couldn't give me any scholarship money that first year."

Brandon was willing to work for it, and so was his dad. "My father paid the tuition for my freshman year," Brandon says. "My life could have gone a whole different way if it hadn't been for my mother and father. Some of my friends went down a wrong path, being in the streets and drug dealing. In high school, basketball physically kept me away from that stuff. I was at practice, on the road. Then I lucked out when Coach Prosser took a chance on me."

After that, Brandon made his own luck. Starting with summer school and working through the next academic year together, Brandon and I devised an academic plan including time set aside for study, tutoring for his classes and help with basic skills, such as note taking, memorization, outlining and summarizing. He worked like a kid possessed—or maybe a kid possessed, for the first time, with the big picture.

Brandon joined the team his sophomore year, playing with future NBA players David West and Romain Sato. The six-foot-five-inch forward never got as much time on the court as he wanted.

"It was embarrassing," he says. "I was sitting on the sidelines a lot. I thought maybe I could make NBA, but God was telling me something else, that basketball was just a stepping stone. I listened," he says. He redoubled his efforts in the classroom, graduating in three years with a bachelor's degree in criminal justice in 2002.

He used basketball to get what he needed. He was led by his faith.

People ask me if I have ever counseled our athletes on religion. I never have. Nobody has ever said to me I'd like to be Catholic too. But I distinguish between religion—what we do in church—and spirituality. I have always sensed a deep faith among athletes. I believe they know they are special, know they have unique gifts. I have used that, not to make them Catholic but to help them get in touch with themselves and with God within themselves.

They can see that I am comforted and made happy and peaceful by my own faith, and sometimes they ask me to pray for them or for someone they are worried about. Sometimes they come to me when they face a crisis, such as a death in the family or when somebody they love is sick or hurt. I love them and want them to be happy, but it is also my job. Worry touches their work. It is very hard to concentrate on a history final if you think your aunt may be dying of cancer.

Matt Stainbrook, Xavier's beefy center, suffered a strained ligament early in 2014, and I knew he was undergoing treatments before a big game. When I saw him slumped in a chair, I reached down and absently made a cross on his knee—almost out of habit. He turned his face up to me and said, "Sister, I needed that."

The best way I have ever found to improve somebody's spirits is simply for them to do something for somebody else.

Our athletes are required to participate in at least one service project each semester. They've volunteered at the City Gospel Mission, Ronald McDonald House and Special Olympics. They've worked with the poor, the elderly, the sick and the young. Father Mike Graham has forged a strong connection with a Cincinnati magnet school, the Academy of World Language, where English is a second language for about half the students. Not surprisingly, this is a great favorite among our bilingual athletes.

Every year at Christmas, the team comes to the convent in Reading. They meet with youngsters from inner city parishes who are each given a small basketball like the ones cheerleaders throw to fans at our games. Each player signs the ball with a silver marker, giving them a natural chance to meet and talk. Matt, who towers over them,

Brandon McIntosh found his purpose far from the basketball court.

is a particular favorite. He is eloquent and gentle. According to one little boy, "This has been the best day of my life."

The athletes read to the children and sit with them during a Mass. I don't know who gets more out of the experience. Well, perhaps I do know.

"People at Xavier sow these little seeds into a person," Brandon said. "It brings about our true purpose. Everyone wants to know their purpose in life, what they are here for."

Now senior pastor at Macedonia Baptist Church in Columbus, Brandon McIntosh is a counselor for troubled youth, a husband, father and volunteer chaplain for the Fellowship of Christian Athletes. He is surely what the National College Athletic Association (NCAA) had in mind when they created their Champs/Life Skills program.

Offered in 1995 as an answer for the graduates who immediately need more than basketball in their post-college lives, the Champs/Life Skills program coincides neatly with the holistic Ignatian values of our Jesuit university. When we heard about it, I applied to get into the program. Jeff Fogelson had approved it with his customary good sense and came up with the money to send me to Overland Park, Kansas, where the association was headquartered. Before the NCAA moved to its spacious quarters in Indianapolis, the office was small and forty miles from the nearest airport, but the week-long session there was impressive.

I shipped twenty-five binders full of programs, regulations and research back to Xavier.

The framework was called the Five Pillars, signifying balance between the five areas of student life. We modified the NCAA plan, adding Xavier's values and resources. Dawn Rogers, who came to Xavier University in 1998 as associate director of athletics, enlarged and strengthened the program. Now at Arizona State University in Tempe, she increased the advising budget and hired additional personnel during her years as athletics director from 2004 to 2006.

Our version, called Student Athlete Development, includes: athletic excellence, academic excellence, personal and social development, career development and leadership through service.

The first one, athletic excellence, doesn't mean simply being a good swimmer or tennis player or golfer. It means training the student-athlete to make good decisions. It means giving him a taste of self governance, of seeing, as Brandon would say, the big picture. Those of us who work with athletes are very used to hearing "coach says." Xavier's Student Athlete Advisory Council (SAAC), which gained traction during Dawn's years, allows athletes to have some say-so as well. Each team elects one delegate and the coach appoints another to the council, which helps devise programs for the five pillars. SAAC also gives them a mechanism to bring complaints and ideas to the athletic and academic directors.

> And when the lights go out on the basketball arena for our athletes, I hope their time at Xavier will have expanded their comfort zone to include theaters and museums and people who don't play basketball.

Besides study hall and tutors, our pillar of academic excellence puts an additional adviser in each athlete's corner. After the departmental adviser prepares the athlete's schedule each semester, it's up to his athletics/academic adviser to help move the student toward graduation. This puts academic goals in the mainstream of the university, undeterred by athletic considerations. At the same time, we acknowledge the rigors of travel and playing a sport while keeping up in the classroom.

The third pillar, personal and social development nudges athletes toward student life. For instance, for five years, beginning in 1995, our summer school program included Shakespearean drama. Joe Wessling, an English professor, produced plays with British colleague, Nancy Nevinson. According to Joe, "Those athletes were naturals because they loved to entertain." Joe remembers two plays performed mostly if not entirely by basketball players: the Pyramis and Thisbe scene from *A Midsummer Night's Dream* and the closing scene in *Of Mice and Men*, in which George shoots Lennie.

"James Posey played Thisbe—a girl—with padded bra etc.," Joe says. "I cannot remember the name of the fellow who played Lennie, but he was powerfully built, about 6 foot 6, and played center on the team. He was excellent in that role."

No wonder we could always count on a big crowd with coaches in the front row of every performance.

Sherwin Anderson, who played basketball for Pete Gillen and Skip Prosser in the mid-1990s, remembers starring in a more contemporary production, *The Colored Museum*, characterized by critics as "fearless humor about black and white America." Nancy Nevinson not only gave Sherwin acting lessons, "she literally taught me how to speak," he says. Fricatives were not part of the patois of Guyana he spoke as a child, and "she taught me to push my tongue against my teeth to make the 'th' sound and to enunciate all my words more clearly. Makes a big difference in this world—how you sound," he says.

"I also loved acting because it gave me a chance to show my happy side."

Players got fine arts credit by participating, by becoming part of a team that wasn't athletic, and with students they probably wouldn't have met otherwise.

It was a class Sherwin took just to please me, I think. Today, he says he used what he learned on stage to land a job as a rep for Nike and later standing up in front of crowds to talk about his youth basketball training program, Sherwin Anderson Skills Academy. He's proud, too, he says, of drawing his basketball students into their communities as volunteers at Ronald McDonald House, Habitat for Humanity and an area soup kitchen. They've helped the homeless, and been involved in fund-raisers to support other programs.

His candid account of his struggles moved the crowd to tears at a Father's Day homily at Phillipus Church in Cincinnati's Over-the-Rhine neighborhood. "Xavier will not let you forget that you have to share yourself."

$\mathcal{B}$esides on-campus projects, we try to make it easy for athletes to take advantage of Cincinnati's cultural riches. Calendars, transportation, sometimes just a friendly tug in the direction of a concert or art exhibit. People are fond of saying, "I don't know much about art but I know what I like." I believe that most of us like what we know. And when the lights go out on the basketball arena for our athletes, I hope their time at Xavier will have expanded their comfort zone to include theaters and museums and people who don't play basketball.

We administer a thorough questionnaire to every athlete to help him identify his off-the-playing-field assets and ways we can help him grow and offer three one-credit courses for personal and social development, such as lectures on nutrition and alcohol and drug abuse. The fourth pillar, career counseling, includes a two-credit course, covering everything from choosing a major to internships.

Richie Harris of the starched shirt and pin-stripe suit and banking internship is now Richard C. Harris, president of his own Dayton-based company, P3Secure, that sells emergency and medical supplies, such as power generators, masks, protective eye wear and specialty foods, to government agencies. When you go through airport security and the TSA worker is wearing blue gloves, chances are they came from Richie's company. After Hurricane Katrina, he consulted with the city of New Orleans to develop better emergency response. When he was a rep for a company that sold funeral services, he was the guy who convinced Costco to include caskets in their merchandise lineup.

"One of the things that helped shape me as a person and as a businessman is what they drill into you at Xavier about helping people," he says. "I think it destined me to choose the way I make a living."

All our student-athletes are connected with mentors and coached with writing resumes and cover letters. They get practical experience, plus they learn many of the "soft skills" so prized by today's human resources departments from their coaches and their fellow players, reinforced by our academic advisers—work ethic, time management, problem solving, learning from criticism, working under pressure, flexibility and communication. Not to mention a positive attitude.

If our development manual had pictures, right next to "positive attitude" would be a photo of Dante Jackson.

Recruited by Sean Miller from Greenville, Ohio, he came to Xavier in 2008. We'd met during an earlier visit. "People had been telling me about this nun who was really strict and organized," he says. "I'm not Catholic, and I was intimidated, didn't think I would know how to act." He acted like himself, and himself is very charming, then and now. I'd never have guessed he was apprehensive.

His grandmother had studied at Miami University, but "then there was a gap. I really wanted to be the first in my immediate family to get a degree."

Right away he stubbed his toe on a paper he had to write for his English class. "I thought I had worked really hard on it, went to the library, did the research, typed it up and still got a D." Dante was discouraged and bewildered. I told him what I knew to be the truth. His professors wanted him to succeed. Find out what went wrong. Build a relationship with your professors, I told him.

He met with the English prof who told Dante that his thinking was good, but the paper was full of typos.

"Hey, I can fix that, I thought."

Dante admits until he came to study at Xavier, "I did what I was asked to do in class. But not a speck more." It's a hard habit to break, but his coaches stayed with him, and so did I.

Dante remembers a trip to the National Underground Railroad Freedom Center down on the Ohio riverfront, part of a class I taught on diversity. "Visiting that place took us away from campus, away from basketball. We saw what people went through to live a better life. My coaches and Sister used to say that they cared about our development as a complete person. I believe they meant it."

When Dante Jackson played basketball at Xavier, he was a fan favorite and leader of a team that saw Atlantic 10 titles and Sweet 16 and Elite Eight appearances. Besides his contribution on the court, he was a one-man cheering section, once hoisting the blue "X" flag for an exuberant victory lap around the court. After graduation in 2011, he went to Ohio University as a graduate assistant. He came back to Xavier, working on his master's degree in sports administration, and as a graduate assistant with the team. He was hired last spring as an assistant basketball coach at Northern Kentucky University, one more rung on his ladder toward coaching his own team. Maybe it will be ours.

"I will always love Xavier," he says. "I love Coach Mack and the staff. Coming back here was like a dream come true. The culture—mind, body, spirit... Even when I was gone, I tried to represent Xavier in the way Xavier's supposed to be represented."

Dante and I were on a game trip together last winter, when he was still working at Xavier. The weather was harsh and there were delays in getting the plane off the ground. Then Dante helped haul the luggage off the plane at Cincinnati's municipal airport, Lunken Field, and onto the bus back to campus. He wasn't wearing gloves.

When we finally arrived at Cintas Center, everyone groaned. The worst winter anybody could remember had just delivered another frigid gift. Our cars were covered with snow and ice. As I was leaving, I could see Dante Jackson across the dark parking lot. Wearing a light coat, still no gloves, he darted around the car of an older woman he'd met on the trip. I could see her try to wave him off. He shook his head and continued to clear her windshield, freeing wipers from the ice, dusting snow off the car's headlights, kicking away a ball of ice accumulated behind one front wheel.

Life skills? Character? The big picture? The secret of happiness? It is that fifth pillar—service to others—that I believe would lead us all, no matter which road we take in life, to a sigh of satisfaction, rather than regret. We make those choices, large and small, every day, moving toward, as Brandon McIntosh says, "our true purpose." Once sampled, goodness is a hard habit to break.

For dinner, Dante had a tepid piece of pizza on a paper plate. After two days, he must have been exhausted. The staff works like crazy on these trips, and it was late. Plus we'd lost the game, which takes the starch out of everybody. He could have slipped right past the woman's car and been home by the time she had her defrosters running. His boss was gone. He'd probably never see the woman again. Nobody would have known. But he stood in the snow in wet Nikes until the windows were safely clear, front, back and sides.

He patted the car's hood, grinned and said she was good to go.

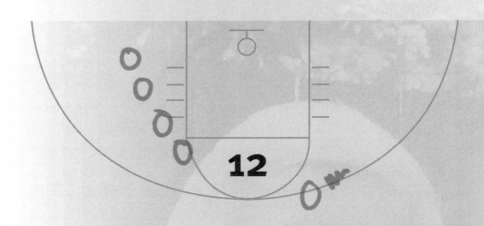

12

A New Mission: Justice

My law degree offered me another way to serve.

Sister Jane Roberts is fiercely efficient. That's the only thing about her that's fierce. Otherwise, she is the most approachable, kindest person I've ever known. She has short, tousled, iron gray hair and an air of welcome. Her quirky sense of humor often comes in handy in our dealings with the law. A paralegal, she is scrupulous, conscientious and patient. She has to be. When someone comes to us for legal advice, she's the first responder, gathering the information we need to get started, usually a couple of hours of cryptic forms, disjointed commentary and painful history.

Together we have taken up the legal cudgel against abusive husbands, negligent moms, deadbeat dads, ruthless landlords and destructive tenants. We have pounded on splintered doors in seedy neighborhoods. We have squinted at apartment numbers in fetid hallways lighted by a single bulb. Jane's middle-aged red Toyota is crammed, her trunk serving as our mobile law office and cat cafeteria. Remarkably canny about people, she is a soft touch for feline strays.

Skip Prosser used to call us the Dynamic Duo. I wish he had seen Sister Jane and me outside the civil and safe environs of Xavier University in pursuit of justice. We are more like Cagney and Lacey without the guns and the smart mouths. Yes, I watch television—my favorite shows these days are *The Good Wife* and *The Bachelor*. I make no apologies. The first one is an authentic legal drama, and, well, just because you have taken a vow of chastity doesn't mean you don't want to know who gets the rose.

I also like the water—swimming and fishing. I play golf and gladly accept invitations to the Cincinnati Symphony and Opera and Playhouse. My work is challenging and fulfilling, but not to the exclusion of everything else around me in this lovely city. Teaching dominates my life, but learning gives me great satisfaction as well.

In 1988, I was awarded my law degree from Salmon P. Chase College of Law at Northern Kentucky University and passed the bar in February of 1989. In May, I was sworn in as an attorney by the late Ohio Supreme Chief Justice John Moyer, who lectured us about service to the poor before we were served punch and cookies and sent on our way to litigate. My brother, Tom, and his wife, Theresa, made the drive to Columbus, as did Sister Jane and Sister Mary Ann Barnhorn. The ever-practical and organized Sister Mary Ann, whose father was an attorney, gave me a number to call for liability insurance, warning, "If people aren't satisfied with what you do, they might find another lawyer to sue you."

Of course, Justice Moyer was not speaking to me personally when he talked about our responsibility to the less fortunate, although he seemed to be looking right at me.

Somebody at Chase had told me in great detail about Volunteer Lawyers for the Poor. Idle conversation. Probably. But even without my black habit, which I had not worn for years, people seem to be able to see what is in my heart. The next day I was insured to the gills, had set up a legal corporation with a $10 balance on the books and was ready to serve the poor.

Now the agency is called the more politically correct Volunteer Lawyers Project (VLP), but it remains true to its original purpose, providing legal services pro bono publico, for the public good, free of charge. I have a friend who says she was really sick once and was really sued once, and she thought getting sued was scarier, more expensive and took longer. Of course, nobody thinks they can remove their own tonsils, but a lot of folks try to handle their own legal work. Mostly because they don't have a choice. Their legal troubles are messy and unprofitable.

The system isn't user friendly. The rules are written by lawyers for lawyers in language that is incomprehensible to normal people. When somebody is caught up in the courts, the process is baffling and frightening. The bogeyman sometimes arrives by certified mail—a summons, a notice that the wheels of justice are grinding in your direction. Whether you like it or not, you have to climb on board, and you don't get to drive.

As Bette Davis said, "Fasten your seat belts, kids. It's going to be a bumpy night." Or many sleepless nights and anxious days. People with money can simply dump their problem in the lap of an attorney and say, "Get me out of this." It might be expensive, but at least they have an expert to guide them. People without money need a similar someone.

Established in 1982 by the Cincinnati Bar Association and the Legal Aid Society of Greater Cincinnati, VLP handles these untidy and financially unrewarding cases. Over the years, they've been joined by attorneys from Butler, Clermont, Clinton and Warren County bar associations.

Everybody has heard the greedy lawyer jokes:

An attorney presents himself to St. Peter at the Pearly Gates. I'm only 49 years old. I'm too young to be dead. St. Peter consults his records and says, "That's odd. According to the hours you've billed, you're 119."

It is worth noting that it is attorneys who keep VLP afloat, not only with contributions to the VLP Foundation but by handling about 1,500 pro bono cases a year in Cincinnati and the surrounding counties. That's a lot of time and money and no billable hours. If people could see some of the misery alleviated by these attorneys, it might take a little fun out of lawyer jokes for them.

Our referrals usually involve family law, but sometimes our clients need help with housing, estate, consumer, employment and immigration issues.

Housing disputes might be anything from a bug infestation to broken plumbing to fire-code violations. We've been on the side of landlords, and we've been on the side of tenants. We've helped families fight foreclosures and save their homes. We've recovered unpaid wages and helped people challenge wrongful termination. We've worked on probate, immigration, Social Security and guardianships. We have handled divorces.

Yes, Jane and I are Catholic to the core, but if a divorce protects an innocent spouse or children from grave physical or moral danger, it is not contrary to Church law. If religious issues arise, we know how to point them in the right direction for help within their own value system or religious beliefs. We have helped women escape beatings and sexual abuse by their spouses. We have protected children from a life where they open a kitchen cupboard and find syringes, bongs and pills instead of Cheerios. A couple of black eyes, children who are cuffed around and terrified to come home are justification for us to enter the fray.

Canon law does not forbid us to handle divorce cases, provided we do not work toward the breakup of the marriage but merely do the legal work after the couple has decided to proceed. By the time the couple gets to us, they are usually way beyond marriage counseling. For the Catholic church to grant an annulment or dissolution of marriage, the parties involved must first obtain a divorce from the civil courts.

Legal Aid screens cases, and their pro bono coordinator refers them to VLP. Legal Aid also covers expenses, such as filing fees, interpreters, copy and transcript services. If money comes our way from non-legal-aid clients, which is rare, we put it in my corporate account and "pay it forward" to help future clients with needs such as food, clothing and school supplies.

I loved my job at Xavier—still do—but figured I could handle a law case a month. Jane would do the time-consuming paperwork and I would step in for an hour or two. Or seventeen. Or a month. Or a year. The dean of the College of Arts and Sciences approved as long as my law career didn't interfere with my Xavier duties. And, thanks to Jane who shoulders much of the burden, it never has.

It didn't take long for us to see that sorting out the turbulent lives of the poor, besides being an emotional wringer, also can be frustrating and time-consuming. A woman fearful of a husband who abuses her may drop out of sight right before she's due in court. Meanwhile, trying to run the offender to ground to serve him with a complaint often means numerous phone calls and many miles on the red Toyota. Sorry to say, we are overjoyed if we find out he is in jail. We know that address.

Sometimes a case comes to us from a former client, another attorney or a judge. In the mid-1990s, a magistrate judge sent us a deaf woman, who claimed to have been unfairly dismissed from her job. She communicated with an odd grunting sound. We found an interpreter in Kentucky who knew sign language and would work for free. We got the company to settle for a few thousand dollars, but when the check came, it was made out both to me and to her. I told her she could have all the money, which I would get to her the next day when the banks opened.

Very agitated, she was suspicious and it was easy to interpret her grunting as a demand to give her the money right now. She shoved us into the car and directed us to an all-night check cashing storefront. I tried to explain that this would cost a chunk of her money. She understood me perfectly. She was very bright but very insistent. As she collected her money and waved goodbye, I knew we would see each other again. And we did.

Since then, I figure I have done about three hundred cases, most from legal aid, and a few poverty cases referred by other attorneys. We represent women in most of our domestic cases. But not always. We spent months getting child-support payments reduced for a barber, whose court-approved payments didn't leave him enough to put food in his own mouth, much less a roof over his head. He was being threatened with prison, so far behind that it was a felony for each of his four children. We wound up calling another barber, an expert witness, who gave the judge a more realistic look at the financial expectations of a man who cuts hair for a living.

Seeking justice for the "poorest of the poor" involves unlovely detail not covered in legal tomes. We have seen soul searing living conditions. We have driven around at night with a mother and her child in the car because she thinks the child will remember where his father works and we need to serve him with a copy of the complaint for child support. We have arranged parenting classes for people, then picked them up, delivered them to the classes and waited to take them home, babysitting for the children in the meanwhile. We have begged judges for continuance after continuance while trying to find wily defendants and skittish plaintiffs who have slipped away between court dates.

At 11:30 one night I got a call at home from a young man who had heard that I might take a "loser" case. His claim was complicated, and it was against a big defendant in Ohio. He couldn't get anybody to listen to him, and he was in despair. He was working in West Virginia pumping gas, had just gotten off work and wanted

With Sister Jane Roberts, keeper of the cat cafeteria and accomplice in a ruthless search for justice.

to come see me right away. I told him to call me when he got close to Cincinnati, and I would meet him at my Alter Hall office. I stuck a pencil in the door so he could get in after hours.

> Maybe she had never heard the phrase "blood from a turnip" or money out of a nun and a night gas station attendant.

He had a long pony tail and a long story. Eventually, I was very glad I listened.

After we filed suit, I received an acrimonious call from the opposing lawyer, who told me I didn't understand the law and threatened to sue me for taking a frivolous case. If I wasn't afraid to meet a stranger in the middle of the night in a deserted building, I certainly wasn't scared of a scolding from a pushy attorney. Maybe she had never heard the phrase "blood from a turnip" or money out of a nun and a night gas station attendant. Experience has shown me that the more another attorney tries to pressure you to surrender, the more you can be certain you are going to win. Besides, thanks to Sister Mary Ann, I was insured to the gills.

The case required regular trips back and forth to Columbus where it was tried. The plaintiff had to drive from West Virginia and, of course, I was driving up I-71 from Cincinnati. A year went by before a judge in Franklin County ruled against us. We appealed. Another year passed while our suit made its way through appeals court. The Franklin County Court of Appeals reversed the lower court's decision. This time, the snooty lawyer made a very nice settlement offer, which my client accepted.

The terms are sealed, but I am allowed to discuss the enormous payment I received. The young man told me: "You have given me my life back." No money exchanged hands between us, but I couldn't have been paid more. It was a cherished moment. If I had been trying to keep a law office afloat with billable hours, I would have had to give up.

Sometimes there is potential for life-changing money, but, as the saying goes, you have to have money to make money. People who come to VLP don't have money to invest in their future—even if they have solid legal grounds. A case was referred to us regarding something called a qualified domestic relations order (QDRO), a legal order after a divorce or legal separation that splits a retirement plan to give the divorced spouse his or her share.

Our client had been married for nearly twenty years to a man who fled the state with his girlfriend. She told us her husband took a big lump sum payment from his retirement plan with him. About $750,000, she thought. She said he also had a large pension. QDROs are not unusual, but the upfront costs of researching and filing the suit and then running the defendant to ground is expensive and time-consuming. VLP and Jane and I cobbled together the money to get started.

> I guess the husband would have liked to have put me out of the "nun business" because he wrote to the archbishop saying I was a disgrace to the Catholic church.

This case took about four years. Meanwhile, our client lost her home to foreclosure and was living hand-to-mouth. When we finally got our day in court, we had an expert witness who testified that the husband had made a fraudulent withdrawal of the money, taking the entire sum without his wife's consent. We won, but if I had been a lawyer hanging out a shingle on my own, no matter how charitable my intentions, this case would have put me out of business.

I guess the husband would have liked to have put me out of the "nun business" because he wrote to the archbishop saying I was a disgrace to the Catholic church. After the circumstances were explained to the archbishop, my superior received a very gracious note from him saying, in effect, carry on with your work. We had nothing to do with breaking up the marriage, but I am proud to say we had a lot to do with putting this woman back on her feet financially.

Another case, which would have broken the back of somebody trying to make a living as an attorney, came through my work with Cincinnati Union Bethel, a non-profit agency which operates apartments for low-income women and preschools for their children. The agency also sponsors Off the Streets, a drug and alcohol treatment program for women. A skein of good souls from law enforcement, medicine, mental health and social services work together to help these women who generally finance their addictions through prostitution.

Since 1990, I have been on Union Bethel's board and was asked to write a will for one of the women living in the agency's historic downtown residence for women, the Anna Louise Inn. She had suffered a stroke and was almost completely paralyzed and unable to speak. Her friends told me she had intended to leave her few possessions to her niece, and they believed that she was distraught by her inability to communicate her wishes.

I spent hours and hours at Alice's bedside. She could let me know what she wanted only by squeezing my hand, so I had to formulate questions that could be answered by one squeeze if yes, two if no. And I had to ask the questions repeatedly, in different ways to make sure I was getting the terms of her will correct. After her death, I located the unsuspecting niece. It gave me great satisfaction to fulfill Alice's wishes, and I hope our time together gave her peace.

Jane and I teach our clients to expect justice and work to help them receive it. Once the legal process is finished, there is so much more to do. Many of the women I represent have no skills, no high school diploma and no income. Once the woman escapes a dangerous marriage, how will she support her children? How will she survive? We try to find her a safe place to live and connect her with someone who will help her take the next step. It might be a GED program or a job.

Sometimes the needs of the disadvantaged seem overwhelming, but I believe God leads us to each other and that our connections are both spiritual and corporeal, with intriguing historic overlaps.

Cincinnati Union Bethel was founded in the nineteenth century for boatmen during the Ohio River's heyday as a busy trade artery. I wonder if the intrepid nuns who arrived at this port from Namur, Belgium, helped with Union Bethel's religious services and Sunday School. When some of the boatmen stayed on here and started families, I wonder if their daughters studied with the "French Ladies."

Congressman Charles P. Taft donated the Anna Louise Inn, named for his daughter, to Union Bethel to provide housing for young women who traveled to Cincinnati from rural areas in search of work. In my heart, I feel sure some of these young women learned geography and history from nuns sent to this corner of the world to carry on the work of St. Julie Billiart, whose order continues to serve "the poorest of the poor" in ways that surely would have surprised and delighted her.

She would love the tiny pizzeria in the Over-the-Rhine area called Venice on Vine, where the food is wonderful but secondary. The real purpose of the place is job training. Just as it is with the poor seeking legal redress, the poor seeking employment are mired in complications. The service at Venice on Vine is sometimes uncertain, but always eager. If soup arrives at the table without the correct spoon, a supervisor whispers and one appears.

I always grit my teeth when I hear people say they don't understand why the poor don't just pull up their socks and get a job. "You see all those help-wanted signs in the windows of McDonald's..." Well, maybe they can't read the sign. Maybe they don't have anyplace to take a bath and comb their hair before the job interview. Maybe they don't know they should come to the interview on time. And it's hard to look perky and capable if you're hungry or have been out on the street all night.

Maybe there is no one who will take the time to whisper a respectful correction.

With $900, Sister Judy Tensing, of our Notre Dame de Namur order, and the late Sister Barbara Wheeler, a Dominican Sister of Hope, started the inner-city restaurant and catering company, one of two businesses operated by Power Inspires Progress (PIP), a non-profit job-training agency, which turns out twelve to eighteen or twenty job-ready employees each year. Trainees are treated with dignity.

And the pizza is very, very good.

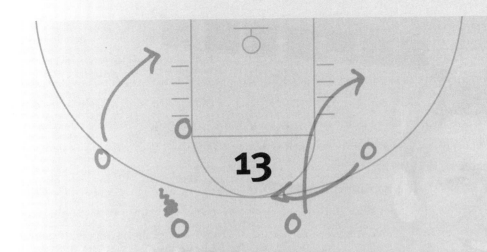

13

Unconventional Methods

Coach Chris Mack, among the extraordinary teaching coaches.

We get complaints now and then about devoting so many university resources to our athletes. Maybe these people should reserve their outrage for the disparity in American schools. Some public schools have indoor pools and film-making equipment, and others have leaky roofs and out-of-date textbooks. It depends on where you live.

> We do not have faculty who will look the other way if a student has a superior jump shot but does not show up for class.

Our coaches look for talent everywhere, from suburbs to the inner city. Every youngster recruited to play basketball for us has at least a high school diploma and either reasonably good standardized test scores—ACT or SAT—or reasonably good grades. We try like crazy to make sure we don't take anybody who can't make it here. That would be cruel.

Xavier is a tough school and frankly proud of it. We do not have a Sub Standard Major with a minor in Sports. We do not have faculty who will look the other way if a student has a superior jump shot but does not show up for class. We do not grade on a curve that includes the trajectory from the foul line.

If an athlete comes here as a high school graduate but without a good high school education, my attitude is now is our chance. And his. I will throw at him every resource we have in this academically rich institution. Everything we've got. I am aided and abetted by imaginative and committed faculty, academic advisers, coaches and administrators. We are in league with each other. We are in cahoots. We collude. We push. We connive. We buttoned-down professors can be ferociously effective when a student wants to learn.

And, in our hearts, we believe they all want to learn. Some of them just don't know it yet.

Take James Posey. He came to Xavier in the 1995-96 season from Twinsburg, Ohio, which is about halfway between Cleveland and Akron. Despite its all-American name, it was a depressed area and James was ineligible to play his freshman year under NCAA Proposition 48 rules. We told his parents we'd help him catch up, but we weren't allowed to give him any tuition money the first year.

His father said he'd take a second job. And he did.

Then it was up to Xavier University and James to get to work. James was both inspired and pressured by his father's sacrifice. He was motivated, but he wasn't happy. He wasn't playing ball yet, and we had surrounded him with tutors, a blizzard of paper, a cacophony of instruction. In our zeal to thrust him into academia, he must have felt as if he'd stepped onto a strange and unfriendly planet. He couldn't do anything right.

When he came into my office, he always removed his hat, and listened quietly, not talking much. One day, his eyes kept drifting to a spot over his shoulder. I finally realized he was trying to read the names on the new basketball team plaque I'd just tacked on the wall. He wanted to see if his name was on it. It was not. This poor young man needed a lift. I made up my mind we were going to talk about something positive.

"James, tell me something about yourself you really like." I expected him to say something like I am really good at basketball.

Instead, he answered, "I am polite. I am respectful. I am a gentleman."

No wonder he was miserable. Besides his athletic ability, he took pride in his behavior. Two strikes against him. He couldn't play ball, and his teachers were asking him to do something, and, polite as he was, he could not comply. My heart went out to this gallant young man, and I wasn't the only one. Tutors, coaches, other students could see how hard he was struggling. Everybody loved him, but the fact remained that he was not up to par academically. Yet.

> I have seen teachers wrack their brains for ideas to repair ignorance and neglect.

The key to James was intense one-on-one attention, tutors re-teaching each subject to bring him up to the level of the rest of the class, telling him things his classmates had heard in elementary school. He never would have made it without grueling remedial training and temporary relief from the demands of basketball. He was smart and had a good work ethic. He needed a new skill set and focus. We revealed to him the secrets of good study habits, using a library, decoding a syllabus. We also went with him when he talked to his teachers, to both give him confidence and to model behavior he could copy. It would have been a lot easier for him if somebody had stepped in sooner.

But, as Father Hoff used to admonish the doubters, "It doesn't matter what they came in with—it's what they leave with that matters."

By the time James finished his freshman year, he had mastered a host of basic study skills and once this guy knew something, he knew it forever. He was in the zone.

Qualifying to play his sophomore year, he continued to be eligible for the next three years and graduated on time, a first for his proud family.

The coach used him as the sixth man on the team. He could charge right off the bench and hit a three-pointer. I used to watch him just as he got to the three-point line. "Why do you shuffle your feet so much?" I asked him.

"That's what I need to do to get the ball in," he said simply.

His physics teacher told me James had figured out the science of a three-point shot. If his feet were positioned in the right way, if his back formed the right arc and if his spine was lined up with the basket, he could hit it. James ranks eighteenth on Xavier's all-time scoring list with 1,455 points and tenth on Xavier's all-time rebounding list with 801.

"I got a good taste of success and winning on the court and in the classroom," he said. "Once you got that taste in your mouth you want more of it."

He led XU in rebounding in each of his three seasons as a Musketeer and earned a long list of honors, including being named the 1998 Atlantic 10 Championship Most Outstanding Player, the A-10's Sixth Man Award twice and was named 1999 A-10 First Team and 1999 A-10 Defensive Player of the Year. He did all of that while rarely in the starting lineup, almost always coming off the bench.

The NBA noticed him.

James was invited to the Green Room, which is not green and it's not a room. It's a place set aside at the NBA's draft site, where the most promising prospects and their families wait to be called on stage—just like behind the scenes at a late-night talk show, I guess. James invited Skip Prosser and me to join him with his family at one of the eighteen tables they'd set up for the players. I was beginning to sweat, then James was picked eighteenth by the Denver Nuggets. There was a lot of hoopla, music and cheering, as he went out on stage and got a team cap.

He played a little over three years with Denver before getting sent to the Houston Rockets, then on to play for the Memphis Grizzlies, Miami Heat, the Boston Celtics, the New Orleans Hornets and the Indiana Pacers. After twelve seasons in the NBA, he's now an assistant coach for the Canton Charge, an NBA development league team in Canton, Ohio, affiliated with the Cleveland Cavaliers.

Talking about his Xavier experiences in later years, James would say, "I always got a sense that everyone at the university was in it together. And after everything my family sacrificed, I didn't want to let them down or be the one to mess up the graduation reputation at Xavier."

He was right. We were in it together, and over the years, I have seen teachers wrack their brains for ideas to repair ignorance and neglect. They were not doing it to preserve Xavier's graduation rate. It's their life's work, a mission. Dr. Bernard Gendreau, who was on the faculty at Xavier for fifty years, presented a paper at the Twentieth World Congress of Philosophy in Boston. His topic: "The Cautionary Ontological Approach to the Technology of Gabriel Marcel." Whew! This learned and internationally known scholar devised a method to explain ancient philosophies to our students using lyrics from popular songs.

Dr. Bill Daily of our communication arts department is known for his innovative independent study programs. Arthur Dewey used to bring his theology students home to dinner with his family, subtly continuing the day's lesson over roast beef and potatoes to make sure they understood what was going on in class. Tutor Betsy Zimmerman cut up textbooks and fashioned her own study guides.

My own foray into the unconventional was after reading a book by Caroline Myss called "Anatomy of the Spirit," who wrote: "Every thought and experience you've ever had in your life gets filtered through chakra data bases. Each event is recorded in your cells." Well, I was aiming for transformation of these young men, not just helping them limp through a few classes. I wanted to unlock their curiosity and send them out into the world ready to connect with the fullness of it. Not just sports, not even just books. This seemed worthy of further exploration.

Excited, I walked over to the library to find a book she mentioned about chakras. I think I was the first customer for this book in a long time. It looked beat up and smelled musty. I'm surprised a moth didn't fly out when I opened it. I read late into the night, hoping to find a new path to understanding these valuable, complicated young human beings who were coming to us.

I did not see this as a quasi-religious experience but as just one more way to try to figure out what was going on in their heads. The seven chakras were a logical spectrum of development, an analytical framework I could use. It was an orderly way of classifying their level of maturity.

For instance, the first or tribal chakra connotes group identity mostly with biological family but it can also extend to tribes we form with co-workers, friends and, yes, athletic teams. Applied to the student athletes, it might be the unbelievable energy that flows from the tribal unity of the Xavier Family as it gathers in support of an athletic event. Translated to a personal level, it might be the extra zip in a child's performance when he or she sees a parent at a soccer game.

The next level is partnership, or moving beyond our tribe to form personal bonds with outsiders. This helped me understand and support a student I'll call Charlie. After his freshman year started, Charlie's mother called to give me the lowdown on her son: that he was poorly organized, had a hard time reading and, among other failings large and small, he was just plain lazy. She had to look over his shoulder every minute. She was convinced that unless someone took her place he would fail. With her guidance, she believed that I could be her on-campus replacement.

Charlie had a better idea. Her name was Mary. She was an attractive nursing major with good grades and a family that sent her off to school without looking over her shoulder. She was well organized, great on detail and did not think Charlie was lazy or a failure. She thought he was handsome. She helped him focus on his studies, taught him better time management and, not incidentally, opened a world beyond his mother. Charlie had moved up the ladder. He didn't abandon his mother—he just made room for other people.

Other chakras or levels correspond to ego and emotion.

> Sometimes, my stomach lurches when I am reminded of what some of our students are up against, the bruising poverty, the bleak world view.

As always, I was enthusiastic and talkative about my new interest. I think it's fair to say that most of my friends and fellow religious thought I was a little nuts. They'll mention karma casually as they step over a bug and mantra when they are discussing diet plans, but if I try to tell them about chakras, they look for the exit sign.

The NCAA has its five pillars, erudite educational researcher Arthur Chickering has his seven vectors of student development and legendary coach John Wooden lectured on the fifteen building blocks of his Pyramid of Success. All of us are searching for more effective systems to apply to learning. So I make no apologies for borrowing wisdom from a 4,000-year-old religion. To me, the seven chakras simply help sort out the vast differences of experiences and maturity of our student athletes. One more tool. Another arrow in our quiver. As Byron Larkin's mother, Shirley, so wisely observed, one size definitely does not fit all.

Former teammates Justin Doellman (left) and Derrick Brown meet up overseas.

Sometimes, my stomach lurches when I am reminded of what some of our students are up against, the bruising poverty, the bleak world view.

After a spring break, I was talking—lecturing probably—to one of our students. His brow was furrowed, and I could tell he wasn't really listening. He had other things on his mind.

"What's the matter, Denny? Missing your family?" I asked.

"It's not that, Sister. I just worry that they don't have enough to eat."

Another boy was sitting next to me on a game trip. He looked out the airplane window as we were landing and wondered, "Look, look, Sister, what is that?" It was a palm tree.

These are the same guys who play ball with youngsters like the ambitious and confident Richie Harris, who came to Xavier from the discipline of a good military school. They sit in the classroom next to kids like Byron Larkin, whose siblings came together every evening for a family meal with plenty for everybody.

Our obligation is not simply to get them a diploma, but to expose them to a fuller life—"to prepare students intellectually, spiritually and morally to take their place in a rapidly changing global society and to work for the betterment of that society," the Father Jim Hoff mantra, if you will. Or "to become people of learning and reflection, integrity and achievement, in solidarity for and with others," as Father Mike Graham likes to say.

$\mathcal{D}$errick Brown was just about to turn his back on "the fuller life." Bright with a good academic background from Chaminade Julienne Catholic High School in Dayton, Ohio, he was as gifted athletically as Brian Grant or Tyrone Hill, but he focused on basketball to the exclusion of everything else. Red shirted during his senior year for an injury, he could have had another year of basketball at Xavier and another year of school.

Coach Sean Miller had announced he was moving to the University of Arizona. "Coach Miller is my guy," Derrick told ESPN. "I'm not going back to school." He'd have enough credits to graduate, he said, then he planned to attend what's called a "big man basketball camp" in Cleveland, sponsored by the Cavaliers. It was a way to sharpen his game and get noticed by professional agents and scouts. Derrick fell prey to a galloping case of senior-itis with an NBA complication.

During the second semester of his senior year, a teacher called to let me know Derrick hadn't been showing up for her class, Business Analytics II. I threw a fit. "She is not going to pass you if you don't do the work. That means that you are throwing away years of work. You will walk out of here without a degree."

I conferred with the professor of the class, hoping for permission for Derrick to retake the class in the summer and take the final exam in time to get his degree. A roadblock came from an unexpected direction.

Derrick's father, a college professor in San Francisco, dug his heels in, not wanting Derrick to miss the camp because he believed it would help launch his career. Of course, Mr. Brown still wanted Derrick to emerge from Xavier with a diploma. Business Analytics II was not exactly a course in which you could cross your fingers and hope to guess the correct answer on test questions. Students definitely needed to do the prep to pass the course.

There was no way Derrick could go to summer school in Cincinnati and attend the camp in Cleveland at the same time.

It was a standoff.

You either did the work and knew the material or you didn't pass. Derrick had the intellectual ability, but he'd missed a lot of class and a lot of information. I was running out of time and running out of arguments. How could I make it clear that he had to do Exercise 129 in a statistics class, even if the NBA was knocking at the door? It was hard to compete with the lure of attending the big man's camp and meeting important sports figures—plus the media and fan attention.

His professor came up with a solution. A qualified adult tutor she knew lived in Cleveland. She said she'd allow one-on-one classes for Derrick while he was at the basketball camp, stipulating that he had to come back to campus to take the final exam. Mr. Brown arranged to rent a room for the tutor to meet with Derrick every day and cover the material. It worked. Derrick passed and got his degree, graduating with the class of 2009.

He entered the 2009 NBA Draft and was selected fortieth overall by the Charlotte Bobcats. He signed a two-year contract, but the Bobcats waived him in 2011. Then the New York Knicks announced they had claimed him off waivers. Late that year, he returned to the Bobcats, then in 2012 he signed with the San Antonio Spurs but did not make the team's final roster. He signed with the Russian team Lokomotiv Kuban Krasnodar in 2012 and was named to the All-Eurocup Second Team in 2013.

I've lost touch with Derrick, but I suspect that this isn't the way he planned for his basketball career to go. I am grateful for the unconventional methods of that resourceful business professor and to the tutor and to Mr. Brown, who made it possible for Derrick to be better prepared for the "rapidly changing global society" with a fall-back position, if he needs it. He'll face his future armed with a college degree.

I am proud of that, and of the many students who have come to our university and left with diplomas. I also dream that we have given them the tools to live a life full of purpose and offered them a look at the palm trees.

Unconventional Methods

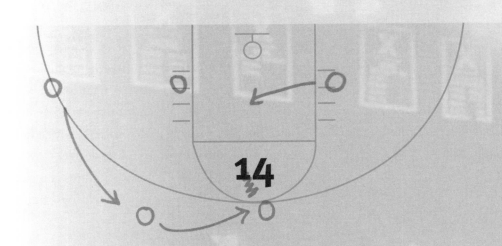

14

Great Expectations

Father Hoff, taking a risk, never saying the
"A-word."

*P*ete Gillen laughs about what it was like to recruit in the days before Cintas Center. "You'd be talking to a kid you wanted and bring him to see where he'd be playing. So we'd stand in Cincinnati Gardens right after a rodeo, and I'd be pretending I couldn't smell horse manure."

Bob Kohlhepp didn't think it was funny. Engaging and congenial—he loved taking Father Jim Hoff out to karaoke bars and singing with him—he strikes me as a man who is serious about the things that matter to him. Xavier matters to him. Basketball matters and winning matters.

When I met with Bob at the Cintas company headquarters, just off Interstate 71 near Kings Island, he didn't send someone to collect me in the waiting area. Right on time, the chairman of the billion-dollar commercial uniform and supply company trotted briskly down the impressive two-story staircase. Trim, tanned and with every charcoal gray hair smoothly in place, he led me on an equally zippy trip back upstairs.

I tried not to look smug when I was not winded.

People have called me relentless. They should have been behind the scenes when Cintas Center was hatched. Bob remembers being in Dayton just after losing a big game to the Flyers, a story he has told many times. "I'm a very competitive guy, grew up with five brothers." He smiles and shakes his head. He was convinced that the cheering Dayton fans gave that team the edge. Just afterward at a reception, he buttonholed Xavier's president, Father Jim Hoff, and Michael Conaton, XU's board chairman.

"We need a facility on campus," he said, weary of following tractor pulls at the Gardens and going to off-campus sites for big events, such as commencement. And then, he said, "I'll put the first million dollars in." He laughs. "I wish it had only cost me a million."

When he was CEO, and "working some crazy hours, Jim and I were golfing at my club and I told him my time was now more important than my money."

"Not to me," Xavier's president responded.

Talk continued about a new basketball arena. "Jim never said yes. He never said no. He never told me to do anything, but he never told me to shut up." They started to get "some push back from faculty, students, from the non-sports enthusiasts at Xavier," questioning the idea of putting an arena ahead of academic needs.

"We stopped calling it an arena. Jim said never to use the A-word." They continued discussions about what those in the inner circle now called a "multipurpose convocation center," with conference rooms, a dining and banquet hall and, ahem, a place to play basketball. "The campus at large still had not bought into it."

Father Hoff was still feeling heat.

Bob Kohlhepp speaks fondly of his years with Jim Hoff. "A great leader. A wonderful guy. If you spent an hour with him you felt like you'd known him twenty years." After an evening with him at the Queen City Club, Bob told his wife, Linda, "I really like this new guy but I'm afraid he's not tough enough. Boy, was I wrong. He was tough as nails, never satisfied, always looking to get better, to do more, to be perfect."

> He was tough as nails, never satisfied, always looking to get better, to do more, to be perfect.

According to Bob, Father Hoff almost took a pass on the job at Xavier. Father Albert DiUlio, president of Xavier from 1986 to 1990, left here to take the presidency of Marquette University. His neck-and-neck competition for the job was another Jesuit from Milwaukee, James E. Hoff. "Our board thought we ought to talk to this Hoff guy."

No, thanks, they were told.

Meanwhile, Michael Conaton, a director of Midland Company, was the place holder, the interim president until they could replace Father DiUlio.

The process of being vetted for a university presidency is grueling, says Bob Kohlhepp. "They have a series of interviews with faculty, with students, with the board." Father Hoff said he'd just gone through all this and had no appetite for more. There was some back channel negotiating with the provincial, in effect Jim's boss. "He wasn't pressured to take the job, I don't think," Bob says. "That's not the way they work. But I think he was encouraged to at least listen to us."

Mike Conaton took his search committee to Chicago, meeting with Father Hoff in a room at O'Hare Airport. Father Hoff flew in from Omaha, where he made the point very clearly that he was comfortable at Creighton University. After a half hour, "Father Hoff excused himself," Mike remembers. "And we realized that we thought we were interviewing him. It was the other way around."

Father Hoff came to Cincinnati to visit on the Reds' Opening Day weekend, said he'd left all his red clothes in Omaha, "so I loaned him a red cashmere sweater I'd gotten for Christmas and hadn't taken out of the box," Mike says. "I never saw that sweater again, but it was sure worth it." He probably forgot. A stickler about so many things, Father Jim was notoriously unconcerned about clothes and was known to make minor repairs—say, a drooping jacket lining—with his office stapler.

When Father Hoff came to Xavier he brought in his own academic dean and others. The only people who survived on Xavier's top staff was the chief financial officer Richard

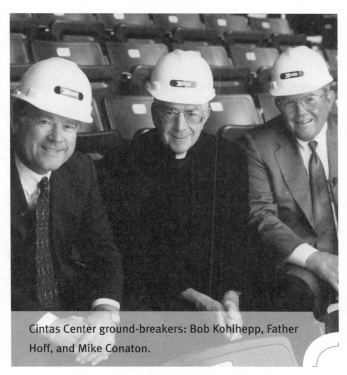

Cintas Center ground-breakers: Bob Kohlhepp, Father Hoff, and Mike Conaton.

Hirte and administrative vice president John Kucia.

At a board meeting, in executive session, Bob Kohlhepp remembers, "I said, we must never, ever let this happen again. We should not have to go outside, ever again, to get our top guy. An organization can't function well that way. Jim Hoff's number one job should be to identify his replacement, get him ready." And he identified Father Graham.

Father Hoff and Bob Kohlhepp developed a solid working relationship and a warm personal one, meeting socially and "arguing about philosophy, politics—everything under the sun." Jim loved music and loved to dance. He was always twirling somebody's wife around the dance floor, according to his friend. His favorite song was Nat King Cole's "Unforgettable." Bob and Linda Kohlhepp still have coffee mugs with Jim's picture and the word "unforgettable" on them.

As plans for the new home for the basketball team seemed stalled by opposition on campus, the two men went to dinner at the China Gourmet in Hyde Park, run by the competent and gracious Bing Moy family, who serve wonderful food and know enough to leave diners in peace with their dem sem and bacon wrapped scallops when they appear to be having a serious conversation. This was a serious conversation, a turning point.

"Jim, give me a straight answer," Bob told Father Hoff. "I believe we need an on-campus arena at Xavier. But, if you tell me to stop talking about it, I will. But until you tell me to shut up, I'm going to keep pushing. And I'm going to push hard."

In March of 1994, Xavier University formally accepted an invitation to move to the Atlantic 10 Conference starting in the 1995–96 school year. This was a big change for our student athletes. The teams were tougher and the games were farther away.

Faculty challenged their boss:

"When are these students going to study? They'll be spending all their time on a bus and in motels. They'll be exhausted." I set up morning meetings with faculty and coaches. They picked at their bagels and cream cheese and talked a bit, grumbling about the early hour. It took Father Hoff to get them on the same page.

He told faculty he'd charter a team plane to get them to games and "back in their own beds" just as if they were going to nearby games on the bus. He said it would also help us with recruiting. Players don't want to spend all their time on the road any more than we want them to. I believe he was looking toward a future when the university would attract students from a bigger pool. He loved basketball, it's indisputable, but I think he saw the sport as essential for the institution's survival.

None of us ever thought his ambitions were for the greater glory of James Hoff. He wanted the best for the institution. Basketball would pay for classrooms and teacher salaries, for dormitories and electronics. He was a true leader, with the confidence to take risks. Calculated risks. But risks nonetheless. I expect somebody warned Dick Farmer's family that their fledgeling Cintas company should stick to rag picking, that trying to swerve over to uniforms might be financially dangerous.

Real leaders can see past what exists to what might be. I've heard it said of good leaders that you can delight them, but you can never satisfy them. That was Father Hoff.

He stuck to his vision and pulled the rest of us along. I was not privy to their conversations, but I believe that he was supported by his board of trustees, just as I was at both schools I led. You depend on staff. You respect staff. But you need outside perspective. I think Bob Kohlhepp was Father Hoff's Bud Koons and Mike Conaton was his Pierce Flanigan. I believe if St. Julie had not been a risk taker, millions of women throughout the world would be the worse. And I think it would have been a lot safer for those Notre Dame nuns to stay in Belgium instead of getting on a ship to a new country.

So I trusted Jim's determination and, yes, courage.

At the same time, I know that Bob kept his word. He was pushing hard with boosters and the donor pool. Jim always called him the "go-to guy" when people asked questions about the center, but I am convinced, and Bob says so as well, that Jim Hoff is the reason Cintas Center was built. Jim had the ability to build the consensus. People respected him and had confidence in him.

Bill Daily of the faculty, who literally taught Bob Staak how to pronounce Xavier, was an early champion of the new center. I am guessing that wasn't a very hard sell.

"Then some others came around, and it was like a ball rolling downhill." Bob Kohlhepp says, "I think we convinced at least the majority of the faculty that, yes, we are an academic institution. We call our kids 'student-athletes,' and student comes first. We should never sacrifice the academics, but we should get both. And basketball can help us."

He cites a marketing survey after Xavier's Elite Eight appearance in 2004. "It was worth $8 million in advertising for us." All three of the Kohlhepp children and two of their spouses chose Xavier, and "in conversations with their friends and a lot of other young people, I was told that basketball is a draw. I think we have to remember that the student is both the customer and the product."

Bob's initial challenge of a million dollars ballooned. "Jim was good at that," he says, half rueful, half admiring. "He taught me a lot about raising money. He recounts three Hoff rules: get the donor emotionally attached, get the right person to do the asking. "Then," and here Bob pauses dramatically, "think big and double it."

When Mike Conaton, a widower, announced plans to remarry, he and his fiance, Nancy, invited friends to the ceremony and reception but insisted that no gifts were allowed. One of Mike's friends called Father Hoff and said in honor of the day, he would like to donate $25,000 to Xavier in Mike and Nancy's names. "He spent some time on the phone with Jim," Mike remembers, "telling him about all the nice things I'd done for him."

Father Hoff's response was typical. "It sounds as if the two of you shared a very special friendship. Don't you think that's worth more than $25,000?"

The Conatons asked Father Hoff to officiate at their wedding, and Nancy presented her husband-to-be and Father Hoff—both notoriously sentimental Irishmen—with monogrammed linen handkerchiefs to carry that day. Father Hoff's homily turned out to be a roast of the groom.

"Hey!" Mike said to his friend.

"I was afraid if I got sentimental I would cry," Father Hoff replied.

One of a kind, our Father Jim Hoff.

Bob Kohlhepp, himself a Xavier MBA graduate, says the First Fund-Raising Rule Of Hoff—emotional involvement—began with two tickets to Schmidt Field House for himself and his oldest son. I don't know how much money Bob Kohlhepp donated personally, but I know he was the single biggest donor, followed by the Cintas scion Dick Farmer and Mr. Farmer's brother-in-law Jim Gardner. According to Bob, "If I raised the most of the three of us, I got to name the building."

The Cintas Center.

"Kohlhepp Center," suggested Xavier's president.

"Nooooo," his friend responded. "Nobody can say it. Nobody can spell it. If it wasn't for Cintas, I wouldn't have the money to give."

So, the $46 million "family room," as Jim persisted in calling it, was officially Cintas Center. The first men's basketball game was played there on Nov. 18, 2000, bidding a final farewell to Cincinnati Gardens in Roselawn, which had been home to the Musketeers since 1983. Before that, they'd played on campus at Schmidt Field House, a first-class facility when it opened in 1928 but with less than 3,000 seats was just not big enough for Xavier's basketball ambitions.

*W*hen Bob Staak took the head coaching job, I remember they spruced Schmidt up a little, painted the floor and the locker rooms. Bob hit the ceiling when he saw his office there, which was about the size of a closet. They moved him and his staff to a bigger space in the O'Connor Sports Center between the soccer and baseball fields.

We were one of the charter members of the Midwestern City Conference (MCC) during Coach Staak's first season after fifty-eight years with no conference affiliation. In 1985, after Pete Gillen came here, it was called the Midwestern Collegiate Conference.

When Jeff Fogelson arrived on campus, I think his marching orders were probably a version of my own at Summit and Trinity: Fill the seats. But first get us more seats. During the Schmidt Field House years, the team had occasionally played at Riverfront Coliseum, but we were definitely in line behind the University of Cincinnati for that venue. UC always had the first choice of dates.

The Gardens, built in 1949, had a distinguished basketball pedigree. From 1957 to 1972 it was home to the NBA's Cincinnati Royals, now the Sacramento Kings. After that, it hosted a colorful and mismatched series of events from monster truck jams to roller derbies, from professional wrestling to motorcycle racing. The Beatles played there. Jeff made a deal with the Gardens in 1983. The Xavier Musketeers were the VIP tenant at the Gardens, but we were still a tenant. Sometimes the team would practice in fleece pants and skull caps because of the hockey ice beneath the floor. Sometimes the air was thick with dust after a tractor pull. And Pete wasn't kidding about the aroma.

The average attendance—less than 2,000 in 1979–80—reached 9,924 in 1997–98, near capacity for Cincinnati Gardens.

The new Cintas Center's arena has 10,250 seats, but, as promised, it also has plenty of room for commencement as well as outside exhibits, concerts, trade shows, weddings and family entertainment events. Its high-tech Schiff Family Conference Center can accommodate gatherings from a small corporate board meeting to a banquet party for 500. The vision of both Presidents Hoff and Graham that Cintas Center become a place for the Greater Cincinnati community to connect, continues today.

There are five levels: event level, dining mezzanine, main concourse, conference level and upper concourse. There's a full-size practice gymnasium, an athletic training room, four full-size locker rooms for men's and women's basketball and for volleyball and visitors, two officials' locker rooms and a media room. The men who would not speak the A-word kept their word.

Nonetheless, no one doubts that men's basketball is the drawing card at Cintas Center. And no one doubts who put it there. "Jim wanted it," Bob Kohlhepp says, "and he was the only guy who could have made it happen." Less than three years after the Dayton conversation, ground was broken.

As the massive, blocky gray complex took shape, Bob Kohlhepp told Jim Hoff he thought he'd like to sing the National Anthem at the first game. "Jim kind of looked at me funny, but then people started coming up to me and asking me about it. It got so far down the road that I couldn't back out." And he didn't want to.

"My wife, Linda, asked me why I wanted to do it," he says, "And I told her because most people wouldn't want to."

Like Father Hoff, Bob wasn't a man to stand on the sidelines. Or to fear taking a risk.

"I thought I could hit all the notes," he remembers, "but I was afraid I'd forget the words." He asked a staffer to put the lyrics up on the scoreboard. Just in case. "I got down on the floor that night. The color guard starts marching out. And the guy who was in charge of the scoreboard grabs my elbow and says it's not working."

He said his wife, Linda, ran up to the family's box suite and hid in the bathroom. She didn't want to be there if he fluffed the "Star Spangled Banner."

He didn't. He hit all the notes. He remembered all the words.

I think probably nobody cheered harder than Jim Hoff. It was a very exciting evening, and I knew we were on our way to a whole new, very demanding world for our athletes.

Bob sang. I took a deep breath. And smelled only the aroma of nachos and pizza with a nice undertone of popcorn.

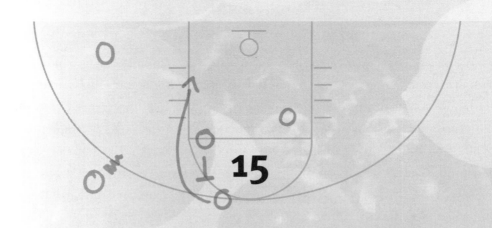

Thad Matta, Epic Teachers

The wonder of it all—David West at graduation.

David West was having a tough night. The acknowledged leader of the Indiana Pacers, he'd been fined $15,000 and ejected from the game for elbowing LA Clippers' Blake Griffin in the jaw. I was at the game, and I didn't see it that way. But I am one of David's biggest fans.

A contingent of us from Cincinnati had driven to the game in Indianapolis during the 2013–2014 season, and we'd invited several area Xavier University alumni to join us for a reception after the game. David West was to be the star attraction. About 250 people were waiting, and we weren't sure he'd show up.

> I think I might have been an acquired taste.

He walked into the room and made a beeline for me, bending his six-foot-nine-inch frame to hug me. Then, in his raspy baritone, he told the room full of people that when he was in school at Xavier, I "kicked his butt." Usually when somebody uses a word other people might not think was appropriate in the presence of a nun, I've noticed they automatically look at me first to see if they're allowed to think it's funny. The crowd was so startled and tickled that they laughed right away, without prior approval.

The truth is, I thoroughly approve of David and have since we first met. He told the crowd he would always be indebted to me, that I put him on the right path and that I was a big part of his life.

I think I might have been an acquired taste.

Bill Daily—Dr. William—was one of David's teachers and describes a love-hate relationship. That is, David loved to play basketball and hated it when I "ratted him out to his coaches" when he wasn't going to class or not earning the grades he was capable of getting. It was never a matter of David not being able to do the work. He was one of the most intellectually able players we ever had, plus he'd had an extra year of high school and strong support from home.

David's family moved from their home in Teaneck, New Jersey, just before his junior year in high school. The boy was soured on basketball. He'd spent most of his sophomore year on the bench and didn't get along with the coach. "It was not a good relationship," his mother, Harriett, says. "There was a lot of cussing. A few of us parents approached the coach about his language, which continued anyway." Amos West says he thinks his son was punished, kept on the bench, because his parents were among those who complained.

"David was really humiliated," he says. Plus they'd all lost respect for the coach. And respect is a very important matter to this family.

Amos retired that year from the postal service, and the Wests decided to relocate closer to aging relatives in Garner, North Carolina, a small town with one high school. It was a good move. David didn't go out for basketball, but it was hard not to notice a six-foot-nine-inch young man in the hallways. Garner Magnet School's Coach Eddie Gray "followed David around, hounded him" his mother remembers, laughing.

"Just come to the gym and shoot around," Coach Gray said. Eddie Gray saw that this kid wasn't just big. He had talent. David took up basketball again. First-team all-state, he took Garner to regional finals, scoring 40 points.

He also was doing better in class, but still dogged by low transfer grades from Teaneck. Coach Gray, suggested he'd have a better chance of playing college ball at a Division I school if he repeated his senior year at a challenging high school with a better basketball team. He could improve his grade point average, as well as his basketball skills, and still be able to play four years of college ball.

"Thank God for Coach Gray," Amos says.

All Coach Gray had to do was convince David's high school English teacher to help him fail, even though he carried a B-plus average in her class. And Judith Darling, the 1996–1997 Wake County (N.C.) Teacher of the Year, consulted with David—several times—and agreed. "It went against everything David and I worked for that year, getting his grades up," Ms. Darling told *Basketball Times* reporter Dustin Dow.

"I wanted him to graduate from Garner," Harriett said, "but Amos agreed with Coach Gray."

David told his mother, "Mom, I'm not ready to play against men."

So, the Wests agreed to send their son to Hargrave Military School in Virginia, about two and a half hours away. It was another good move.

"I was glad Amos insisted," Harriett says. "David grew a lot at Hargrave."

The redoubtable Jeff Battle, who was so effective with Lenny Brown, scouted David. He and Skip Prosser started sitting in the stands at David's games, watching him peel rebounds off the backboard with his gigantic hands. They met with David's parents.

"Coach Prosser became part of our family," Harriett says. "Even today, when I mention his name, I get kind of emotional. That's how much he meant to our family."

The Wests drove to the Xavier campus during the early spring of 1999, his senior year. "The president of the university, Father Hoff, came to us, came out of his office and across the campus to meet us," Amos says. "That really meant a lot." Then he laughs and says, "It also looked like the whole freshman class came out to see David."

I met with David and his parents, and it was clear that they were looking for more than a place for him to play basketball. They asked probing questions about the academics. Not for the first time, I was proud to tell them of our 100 percent graduation rate for our senior basketball players. David received some extravagant genetic blessings. Harriett is six feet tall, and Amos is six-foot-five. Both of David's parents had a shrewd idea of what their son should be able to command from a college interested in his athletic skills. David said after college he wanted to stay in athletics and we talked about majors that might interest him—sports marketing and sports management and communication arts. He says he remembers me as "stern but compassionate."

"It rained the whole weekend, but we liked everything else about Xavier," Harriett says. "I was convinced that they cared for David my son not just David the basketball player. My husband and I are Christians, and we felt at home with the culture on campus."

David signed with Xavier and was put in the starting lineup as a freshman. Skip Prosser was thrilled with him, said he was "something special."

And he was. But not in the classroom. Not yet. Smart as he was, well educated as he was, he still struggled. The players are almost always surprised by how difficult it is, and David was no different. Listening to the recruiting coaches sitting on their living room couch is not full preparation for coming to Xavier. They don't understand what an enormous drain of time it will be to plunge into Division I basketball while keeping up with their studies.

We get them started on the academics, and then the coaches get them to do extra weight lifting and extra conditioning. College is harder than high school, most any high school. Suddenly instead of living down the hall from their parents, they are living in a city of people their own age. Their mother does not look under their bed for a missing tennis shoe or remind them to get to bed early on a school night. There are a lot of distractions.

Reality sets in.

"When David was being recruited, we heard a lot of promises from Coach Prosser and Sister and even Father Hoff about how things would be if David came to Xavier— not about basketball but about his studies," Harriett says. "They kept those promises, went beyond them."

In my weekly meetings with David, I kept looking for something that would galvanize him. We talked a lot. Besides conferences in my office, we ran into each other around campus. In fact, he lived right across the hall from me. A leader on and off the court, David was a magnet for his teammates, who often gathered in his apartment. I could hear him playing his electronic keyboard and singing. On my way out of my apartment, if I could hear him singing in a joyful falsetto, I knew it was going to be a good day, that he was happy.

He told me he'd read about Michael Jordan's basketball camps. He was intrigued, enthusiastic. That triggered an idea. Why not create an independent study course that would allow him to learn how to create, manage and market a basketball camp? Bill Daily, who had David in one of his communications classes, devised a three-credit course, outlining the steps to running a basketball camp for children, including marketing, management, finance, personnel. I knew David would be interested. He would have to find answers to questions such as: When you put together a summer camp, what do you call it? How do you market it? What grade levels should attend? What skills should be taught? How much do you need to charge to make it profitable?

David did, in fact, love it. He created a complex database and took it very seriously. He obtained real knowledge and guidance from a variety of experts. The expert at the top of the list was Coach Thad Matta, which I believe was a significant key to David's future with Xavier.

Skip Prosser left for Wake Forest after David's sophomore season. His replacement was Thad Matta from Butler University in Indianapolis. The son of a high school coach and athletics director, 33-year-old Thad was the ninth youngest coach in Division I basketball. "Mike Bobinski, the athletics director, told the team he would get somebody top-notch in to replace Coach Prosser. And he did," David says.

Thad Matta hears ominous news from a star player.

The Wests—all of them—were crazy about David's first coach, the one who had come to Garner, North Carolina, to sit on their couch in their home and tell them about Xavier University. "We were impressed with Coach Matta also, but the relationship was just totally different."

I've watched our players with their coaches. I believe that for an athlete, the coach is the biggest person in their campus life. The rest of us are satellites orbiting around them. A change in coaches can be troubling. "I actually wanted to leave with Coach Prosser," David says. "But he said that's not the right thing to do. He told me much as he loved me, he loved Xavier University just as much. Everybody told me that Coach leaving wasn't personal, just business."

Bill Daily's independent study course for David led him to a summer internship with Thad Matta's Basketball Camp, working with children and visiting many coaches, including Xavier's new head coach. Thad, like all the head coaches I have seen in my years at Xavier, is an amazing teacher. I have learned so much from watching them with their players and am reminded of a Chinese proverb:

"I hear and I forget. I see and I remember. I do and I understand."

David shared with me some of the training drills Coach Matta used during his internship. The carefully typed instructions are accompanied by elaborate drawings of player movement and strategies with crabbed, handwritten notes, "1–2 Step on catch. Moves off triple threat."

Most of the drills are incomprehensible to me, but clearly by the time these children left the camp they had heard, seen and performed drills that would stick with them for a long time to come. I think perhaps David and Coach Matta forged an important relationship that lasted as well. David could see how much Coach Matta knew. Respect. A very large item.

"I saw David mature," his mother says. "Before he went to college, he didn't particularly care for school. I saw his love for the books increase. He became an avid reader." After the camp, David wrote several insightful papers about leadership, which I still have today.

Meanwhile, he was just a terrific player. In the starting lineup every year, he was honored by the Atlantic 10 as Player of the Year. He could do everything—score, rebound, block shots. And, of course, he was a real team leader.

None of this escaped the notice of the NBA.

A week before the April post-season athletics banquet in 2002, he went home and told Harriett and Amos he wanted to enter the NBA draft. He'd already told Coach Matta he'd be leaving Xavier at the end of his junior year. That must have been wrenching news for the coach. Together they'd had a very good year.

Thad had been named 2002 Atlantic 10 Conference Coach of the Year, leading the Musketeers to the top regular season finish in the league at 14–2 and an Atlantic 10 Conference Tournament championship. Coach Matta became the only first-year coach in conference history to win both the A-10 regular season and tourney championships.

Amos came to Xavier for the annual basketball banquet. "Father Hoff kept following me around that night, asking me what David was going to do. 'Is he really going to leave us?" Amos didn't know. "I really didn't. David surprised us all."

The young man announced at the banquet that he was going to stay at Xavier for his senior year. "The people there clapped for what seemed like forever," Amos says. "I don't think there was a dry eye in the house."

After he made the announcement, David had a Xavier blue "X" tattooed on his bicep. In 2003, he became the first Musketeer to win the AP Player of the Year, was named Atlantic 10 conference Player of the Year for the third year in a row, United States Basketball Writers Association National Player of the year, the Oscar Robertson Trophy and Lowe's Senior Class Award winner, recognizing him as the nation's top senior men's basketball player.

> **Once again, a hero's heart beats beneath a numbered jersey.**

No wonder Xavier retired his Number 30 while he was still playing for us.

During this time of emotional and taxing athletics, David continued to grow as a student. He went to class, earned his credits and studied harder than he had to, completing his bachelor of arts degree in communications by December of his senior year and enrolling in a graduate program in counseling the final semester.

Drafted by the New Orleans Hornets in the 2003 NBA draft, David showed his mettle after Hurricane Katrina decimated the town of New Orleans in 2005. He threw his considerable intelligence, energy and national profile into helping families there. "The devastation was incredible," he remembers. "The most eye-opening thing for me was the massive displacement, the number of people who were helpless, homeless. I am in a position to do something for people. So I do."

Once again, a hero's heart beats beneath a numbered jersey.

Sports Illustrated featured David in its NCAA All-Decade Team, and he joined the Pacers in 2011 for a two-year deal reportedly worth $20 million. "David is the glue that holds the Pacers together," says his ex-teacher Bill Daily. "In Indy, they call him 'the professor' because he is always reading." Professor West recorded his first triple-double

When the NBA came calling, David West put them off for a year, then inked an indelible promise.

with 14 points, 12 rebounds and 10 assists in January of 2013 and re-signed with the Pacers for a three-year contract worth more than $36 million.

Off season, he works with his brother, Dewayne West coaching a youth basketball team. Amid many worthy causes tugging at the sleeve of an NBA star, he says he is most drawn to helping youngsters, well aware of the basketball carrot and stick. "No books, no ball," he tells them. "My brother and I call it 'butting in.' We work with them all along the way—getting in touch with their teachers and principals—anything we can do." He tracks their academic progress, inspects their report cards and keeps in touch—even during the NBA season, ferreting out scholarships, recommending books.

David and his wife, Lesley, have children of their own, a daughter, Dasia, and a son, David Benjamin. He told a *USA Today* reporter that he has never "bought into the NBA lifestyle. I'm not part of that bling-bling culture."

Besides the blue carpe diem letters tattooed on the backs of his legs in memory of Coach Prosser, he has other indelible memories. "There was a need in my life for someone like Sister Rose Ann. She put me on the right path, and I'm always indebted to her for that," he told the Xavier boosters that night last winter in Indianapolis. "So many things go on in your life. You cannot get those small moments again, people that impact your life. You know that without them, things may have been different."

I take pride in the success of David. I'm flattered by what he has to say about me, but he also credits what he calls the "environment" of Xavier University as a "place where you know you will get an education." David arrived here equipped for success, with people behind him who pointed him in our direction.

Others arrive in academic poverty. One young man was placed in special education classes in high school so he would "pass" his classes and be eligible to play basketball. He had neither a learning disability nor was he a special needs case, except that he was a terrific basketball player who didn't like to study. I am proud to say we academics rallied, plied him with tutors and extra attention and dogged him until he was able to master the curriculum here. It was difficult for us, and very, very difficult for him. He graduated with a profound shift in attitude and is standing on the edge of a very successful life.

Romain Sato, who was adopted by a couple in Ohio as a teenager, came to us billed as someone who was fluent in six languages. A native of the Central African Republic, he was actually fluent in one language and knew a lot of words in five others. Romain Guessagba-Sato-Lebel spoke Sango, the language of fewer than five million people worldwide. And one in Cincinnati, Ohio.

The written history of Sango dates back to French missionaries, so a lot of the words in Romain's native tongue are French, and he was using a French-to-English dictionary to painstakingly translate his lessons. Word by word. When I found out what he was doing, I located a tutor to help with his immediate needs and went to see Margaret McDiarmid. When I think about faculty at Xavier who have thrown themselves headlong into the academic fray for these young men, Margaret always comes to mind.

A French professor, she was touched by Romain's story. "I pray that God has a plan for me," he told her, "and that I can help my family." He still had relatives living in poverty in Central Africa. Moreover, he was keenly aware of the turbulent politics there. He dreamed of playing professional basketball or getting a good job and sending money to them.

"His work ethic was incredible," Marg says. "It was enormously time consuming, but I think we were all taken by this kid. He just refused to fail." Romain majored in French, and had "tons of support, tutors, other students, other faculty."

Graduating on time with a major in French, Romain was selected by the San Antonio Spurs in the 2004 NBA draft and subsequently waived. Since then, he has played for teams in Italy, Spain, Germany and Greece. Marg, who recently retired, took a Romain Sato nesting doll with her when she left.

One young man, a terrific athlete and a pretty good student, just could not wrap his mind around fractions. His teacher explained. And explained again. The student, I'll call him Dwight because I know he is still embarrassed about this, just shut down. He did not want to go to class. He did not want to hear another lecture. I kept thinking of the children I saw working with their colored wood blocks in Montessori class at The Summit.

I knew better than to show up at Dwight's apartment lugging a box of red and blue kiddie blocks. It would have been humiliating and a reminder that he couldn't manage to learn something that most sixth graders had mastered. But I suspected he needed to learn this by touching and feeling the physical pieces of the whole. So, I bought four six-packs of soda.

We stacked the cans and grouped them into halves and thirds and fourths and sixths. It worked like a charm. Then we drank the pop.

Another student, someone I will call Jimmy, was recruited from a junior college, where he had completed his freshman and sophomore years. I knew we were in trouble when he came to my office and said, "Where am I supposed to sit?" He had a class schedule, and I thought he was confused about the location of the building. I took a look and said. "I'll walk you there."

He looked mystified and said, "Oh, I know where it is. I don't go to class. I'm special. I sit with the counselors." He was special all right. He'd spent six years in high school—"they rolled me back," he explained—then played for two years at a junior college. We discovered to our horror that this young man could neither read nor write. He could fake some things, picking up on cues, paying special attention to pictures on signs, for instance. But he certainly could not have really fooled a high school teacher or a college professor.

It was shameful.

"It was not that Jimmy had trouble with comprehension, couldn't understand what he'd read," says Betsy Zimmerman, the adept and resourceful tutor we hired to work with him. "He did not know the alphabet, couldn't sound out words. We had to start from scratch." Betsy was a reading specialist, who had worked successfully with several adult illiterates. She had a terrific ally. Jimmy himself.

Mortified that he could not read and weary of the stress of pretending, Jimmy "would do anything I asked of him, was hungry to learn." Betsy literally had to show him how to hold a pencil. She scoured the library and bookstores to find books for him. "I didn't want to humiliate him with kiddie books. Bible stories were great," she says. "He loved them. They were familiar." She found stories about UCLA coach John Wooden that appealed to him. She clipped out newspaper stories, copied poems. She sliced the spines off his textbooks and fed them into a talking word processor/scanner she'd borrowed. She read to him for hours.

By dint of the strategies she had learned and inventing a few others, they made progress. Astonishingly, in one year, Betsy taught him how to read and write. He was working hard and had a lot of people rooting for him. His history professor came to my office as soon as he'd graded Jimmy's final test. "He did it! He passed. He even answered an essay question."

"Did you see him do it?" I asked, mindful of a lifetime of "coping skills."

"Yes. He did it right in front of me."

Father Graham told us to continue to do whatever was necessary and approved an unusually high number of tutoring hours. I checked in frequently with Betsy and his professors. Of course, I kept talking to Jimmy, about his studies, about life, about Chinese food, which he said he'd never tasted.

"When you graduate, I'll treat you to a Chinese dinner," I told him.

It should not have come as a surprise that his exertions as a student would sap his energy for anything else. There are only so many hours in the day, even for the young and eager. Things were not going well on the court. Jimmy decided he had to leave Xavier. When Betsy heard, she wept and called me to come over to the McDonald Library where she was tutoring Jimmy.

"You do not have to go," I told him. "You can stay to graduate at Xavier. We will continue helping you, no matter what."

Jimmy, looking at me, said with great conviction: "Sister, I don't want to stay if the coach does not want me. Do you know what that feels like?" It was inevitable that he would depart.

Sister Jane and I invited Jimmy to join us for a Chinese dinner. Not a celebration, as I had planned, but a very sad farewell with an acrid whiff of failure.

Jimmy tried to cheer me up. "Sister," he said, "you don't know what it was like for me before I came here. I was embarrassed. It felt like I was always lying. I couldn't even go to a bank or get a bill at a restaurant without wondering if I was being cheated. I was scared people my age would find out and laugh at me."

He said he was excited about the future. He said we had changed his life. I try to imagine how his life came to such a pass. Inattentive as a child, maybe moving a lot, missing school and coming back to find that everybody was ahead of him? He had pride, so maybe it was then that he began the elaborate pretenses that Betsy called the "downward spiral." Whatever it was, somebody should have intervened long before he had sixteen years of school.

A success story? I still don't know, although I believe he is better off through the "intervention" at Xavier. We have lost touch. I hope someday, Jimmy and I can sit down over a big helping of Kung Pao chicken, and I can hear how things have turned out for him. The center of our enterprise is to help each individual to become his or her personal best. It isn't simply to get them a degree or a job or an NBA contract. We want to help them live a better life, to know why God made them.

When they named David West Player of the Year in 2003, the editors of _Basketball Times_ called him "the nation's most complete college player." Bill Daily thinks he was even better than that. "When David left Xavier, he was a complete person, a full human being."

That is my idea of success.

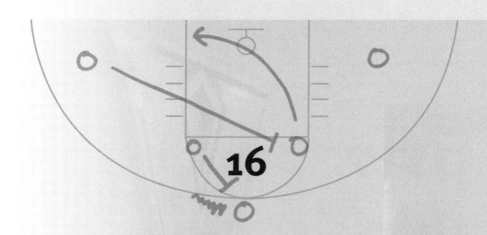

Sean Miller and the Comfort Zone

On the road, challenging players with a
bigger experience.

Sean Miller stood at the door of my office holding a bouquet of flowers. He was leaving to take the head coaching job at the University of Arizona. This gesture was so typical of Sean. He could have just slipped out. It would have been easier, but I never saw him choose easy instead of right.

I loved the flowers but hated to say goodbye.

One of the first things Sean did when he was named head basketball coach at Xavier in July of 2004 was to pay his respects to Father Hoff, who was desperately ill. "I wanted to make sure he was good with me being the new coach," Sean says. "He told me change was good, a chance to shoot for a higher level." It must have been a difficult visit. At the end of Sean's visit, the man who led Xavier University so forcefully could barely speak. His final message to Sean was to extend his hand, palm downward and lift it, a clear upward expectation.

Sean is accustomed to high expectations. His brother, Archie, is head basketball coach at the University of Dayton and before that was Sean's associate coach at Arizona. Their father, John, took four state titles when he coached high school basketball in southwestern Pennsylvania and has a reputation for being strict and demanding, making his sons dribble their basketballs for miles and shoot endless free throws. Sometimes they had to shovel a foot of snow off the driveway first. His senior year in high school, Sean made 93 percent of his free throws.

A young, admirably poised Sean Miller is preserved on YouTube. At age 14, he chats comfortably with Johnny Carson, who clearly likes the boy. After that, Sean shows off his ball handling, a demonstration of what happens when a young person has God-given talent and a father who makes him bounce a basketball wherever he goes—around the house, to school, into restaurants. At an All-Star game in Wichita, Kansas, Sean made fifty free throws in a row during halftime. The "Wizard of Westwood," UCLA's coach John Wooden, asked the youngster for an autograph.

He played for his father's team at Blackhawk High School, averaging 27 points and 11 assists per game. John Miller told ESPN's Rick Reilly, "I never really patted Sean on the back. Never once. If he scored 35 in a game, I'd be on him about his defense."

Bob Kohlhepp, talking about Father Jim Hoff, said, "He was a great leader, never satisfied. Always wanting more." By that reckoning, Mr. Miller certainly qualifies as a great leader. Sean, too, I think.

Sean went on to play point guard for the University of Pittsburgh, then was an assistant for two seasons at Miami University of Ohio under Herb Sendek, along with another assistant coach, Thad Matta. After returning to Pittsburgh for a season, he went to North Carolina State, then joined Thad at Xavier. He lived with the Mattas while he and his wife went house hunting in Cincinnati.

Famous for his winning ways and inspirational quotes, Coach Wooden said, "A coach is someone who can give correction without causing resentment." He could have been talking about Sean. A stern taskmaster when he was running Xavier's team, he also had that indefinable spark of leadership that drove the team to work hard for him without draining their enthusiasm. I think he understands not only basketball but the young men who play the sport.

Thad Matta's departure from Xavier to Ohio State was very abrupt and blind sided some of the players. Even though they all knew Sean as Coach Matta's associate head coach for three seasons, the new head coach was looking for a bonding experience. When the team got a chance to go on an NCAA-approved trip to the Bahamas to play basketball before the start of the season, Coach Miller put them on a plane.

Sean included me as a "monitor," but I swam and played along with everybody else, monitoring a really splendid experience and, making sure nobody ate too much seafood or got sunburned. Basketball. Blue ocean. A beautiful hotel. Exotic food. Water slides. Miniature golf. What more could we want? A dose of reality, according to Sean, who gave the team a choice of spending a service day in a hospital or a prison. To my surprise, they chose to visit a detention center for juveniles.

When we arrived at the compound, a short bus ride from the hotel and eons away from the life we'd been leading for the past few days, the team was subdued. The buildings were surrounded by ugly fencing and menacing coils of barbed wire. The buildings were spartan. We could see the yard, which was muddy, not a blade of grass. Both boys and girls, probably ranging in age from about 10 to 15, were lined up. They were wearing thin uniforms. Our athletes divided the children into teams and showed them some basic ball handling skills, playing for about an hour. Then they started to talk.

"As I recall," says Justin Doellman, who came to Xavier from Ryle High School in Union, Kentucky, "I expected kids with a chip on their shoulder, but they were eager to talk and pose for pictures with us." I was proud of the way our students worked to connect with these children—some of them revealing with raw honesty mistakes they had made in their own lives.

The last time I heard from Justin, he was playing for Valencia BC in Spain, after three years with a French team. He'd just been named to the All-Eurocup First Team, which he

Sean Miller, great on detail, pushing for perfection on the court.

didn't mention in his e-mail. Instead, he wrote that he and his wife, Meredith Frendt, a 2006 Xavier graduate, had just learned they were going to have a baby. He says I "set the stage" for his marriage. Justin had come to me at the beginning of his sophomore year to tell me he had found a girl, a soccer player, who would help him study. Could I help them coordinate their schedules?

I could. Justin had made dean's list his freshman year, and I admired the work ethic that enabled him to contribute to the team and keep up with his studies. Now, it seemed, he was adding another vital facet to his college life.

Like Justin, Meredith was a fine athlete, who wound up a four-year letter winner and captain of the women's soccer team. A liberal arts major, she had a dazzling smile and a game-winning foot. Plus, she was on the Atlantic 10 Commissioner's Honor Roll three years in a row, so I believe him when he says she actually did help him study.

His teammate Brandon Cole also remembers that time in the Bahamas with the sobering side trip. "People tell you you are lucky, have advantages," remembers Brandon, who was an outstanding high school player before he was recruited by Coach Matta, "and you think yeah, yeah, yeah. Suddenly there it is—right in front of you. And you know. I was lucky. I had people around me who cared. I had a talent people would pay me to use. I don't know what kind of life these kids had, but it didn't look good. They seemed very bright, but you didn't get the idea that any of them knew what would happen to them next."

Brandon grew up in a small town outside Chicago, raised by his grandparents, Mike and Diane Flowers. Diane came to see me a lot while he was at Xavier, worried about Brandon, and rightly so.

"I struggled horribly my freshman year," Brandon says. "I almost got kicked out. I was red shirted, I wasn't playing. It was my first time away from home, a difficult adjustment. I really got behind the eight ball. Coaches wouldn't even let me practice until I got my grades up. I would just run the steps at Cintas by myself. I started meeting with Sister."

It was not magic. It was certainly not all me. It was our, by now, time-tested program. Study hall, tutoring, class attendance, family encouragement, structure and a harsh glimpse into life without the team. Brandon was back on track by the time we made the trip to the Bahamas. He played in 93 games in his Xavier career and graduated in 2006 with a bachelor's degree in criminal justice. Drafted in 2007 by the Chinese team, the Xingiang Gyanghui Flying Tigers, he has since played in Kuwait, Japan, Brazil and Saudi Arabia. He was also in Macedonia for a season.

He's now on the Issa Town roster in Bahrain, a small island country near the western shores of the Persian Gulf. Skype, the friend of traveling parents, keeps him in touch with his young daughter and son back in Cincinnati. "I miss home, but it's beautiful here," he says. "I have teammates from all over the world. Everybody has a story. I try to soak 'em all up. It makes you a better overall person, and it makes you comfortable, no matter where you are or who you're with, whether it's an oil sheik or a police officer or a CEO of a big company or a construction worker."

I can still see him as a young man in that bleak prison yard in the Bahamas, talking to youngsters about making mistakes. "You can start over," he told them.

Standing next to Brandon that day was teammate Justin Cage, who has been playing in Belgium for the past six years after bouncing around the United States on NBA development teams. "When I first came to college, I had trouble with everything, with the courses, with time management, with basketball. I was not the best student," he says. "But they stayed with me, no matter how long it took."

He remembers driving through a rough section of the Bahamian country, "not the tourist part, very bad areas," and told the children at the detention center about his own experiences, speaking passionately about education, urging them to study, telling them to "play by the rules." Turning down Butler, Ball State and Memphis, Justin came to Xavier from Indianapolis, where he was named Indiana's Mr. Basketball 2003 by the *Indianapolis Star*. "I wanted to play for Thad Matta," he says. "When he left, it bothered me a little, but Coach Miller was right there, and we knew each other."

Coach Matta and Sean have very different styles. Thad did everything himself, directing the entire operation. Watching him, I became aware of how much all five players had to work together, that it was not enough to know your own skill and your own game, you had to know your teammates. Under Thad, the assistants were more like support staff. Sean, on the other hand, involved the assistants in coaching and drilling. He was great on detail and pushed for perfection. He reminded me a lot of Pete Gillen.

Like Pete, who sometimes thought I pressed them too hard on the academic side, Sean was always aware that his players were young, still growing and unformed. He made sure they didn't get lost on trips, didn't get hurt. That said, he could be ruthless about their physical training. Some of the players got a taste of John Miller's early regimen for his sons, a hundred free throws before breakfast. I saw him make players push a plate across the floor with their noses, run and run and then run some more. But I never heard a complaint or a derogatory remark from the players. I supposed there was a reason, and I guess they supposed the same thing.

They—and everybody else—could see that Sean knew what he was doing. After our trip to the Bahamas, Coach Miller took the Musketeers to four NCAA tournaments, in addition to winning three Atlantic 10 regular season championships and one conference tournament

> I believe his character had an impact on his team that went beyond what they learned on the basketball court.

championship. In the 2008 NCAA tournament, the third-seeded Musketeers were eliminated in the Elite Eight by UCLA, which was seeded number one, and in 2009, they were eliminated in the Sweet 16 by another top seed, Pittsburgh.

"The hardest decision I ever made was to leave Xavier," Sean says. "It's an incredible place. I'm Catholic, and when we moved to Arizona, my wife and three boys became Catholic too, in no small part because of our experiences at Xavier, the people we met. The process began there." He gives me a large measure of credit for his family's

Sato helped lead Xavier to a school record high 12th in the final Associated Press Poll in 2002.

conversion, which I gratefully accept. What has brought me so much joy and peace I would surely wish for his wonderful family.

When Sean came to say goodbye, I thanked him for his work with us and said it must be time for him to make a difference in another place. He certainly was a talented and effective coach, but I believe his character had an impact on his team that went beyond what they learned on the basketball court. He left an enduring impression with me as well. That Caribbean trip had an unusually strong effect on me, very spiritual, seeing these young men respond to the children they met and watching their awakening about how others live.

Margaret McDiarmid, who made such a powerful change in the life of Central African Republic native Romain Sato, has arranged several study trips abroad for our student-athletes, giving them, as she puts it, "a bigger view of the world." At Xavier, I was surrounded by an enormous wealth of worldly experience, our excellent faculty, and I capitalized on those riches. Sometimes I wonder that the faculty did not hide under their desks when they saw me coming. Whatever they were already doing for our students, I always had a notion of something else. And they never let me down.

When I proposed a Faculty Athlete Mentor Program at a Xavier University faculty meeting, I showed up with graphs, slides, charts and my customary optimism. Some of my optimism no doubt stemmed from my experiences thirty years earlier at Trinity, when Sister Barbara Brophy of our counseling center worked with Trinity's expansive base of alumnae in what she called a "partnership of learning." It was a flexible starting point for career development, and many jobs and internships resulted from the interaction of students and alums. But a significant by-product was a deeper connection between participants.

Although Xavier's students and faculty have good interaction in the classroom, I believe they still have a lot to learn about each other. I was not looking for career opportunities. I was looking for ways to improve understanding between athletes and their teachers. Nearly every freshman I've met is scared to death of professors and has a terrible time asking questions or setting up conferences, even though better communication would make it easier on everybody. And not surprisingly, most faculty have only a vague idea of the life of a student-athlete.

First, I ran the idea past the coaches. If they weren't on board, I knew I was dead. They approved the concept but wondered if faculty would make the time commitment. Deep down, I wondered as well. I wanted to assign at least one faculty mentor to each of our athletic teams, somebody who would come to team meetings, be available to coaches for consultation and reach out to at-risk athletes. I wanted faculty to see what these athletes do for their scholarships. I suggested they might occasionally invite athletes to their homes for meals, talk with them about campus resources and career opportunities, attend the end-of-year All Sports Banquet and participate in NCAA-allowable recruiting activities, such as meeting with their families on campus visits.

It meant a lot of additional work—sort of like hiring a surgeon to remove somebody's appendix, then asking her to come back every day on her own time to change the patient's dressings, plump up the pillows and fix a meal.

I wasn't fooling anybody—nor did I try—it would be time-consuming and unpaid. At most, they'd get a hat or tee-shirt. Some faculty actually followed me out of the room and into the hallway, sign-up sheets in hand. I had been worried that I might get takers only for the most visible sports, that it would be like pulling teeth to get anybody to sign up for, say, golf or track. By the end of that week, I had mentors for all eighteen sports and a waiting list. This was Xavier University at its best.

"Sometimes the game is the highlight of my day," insists Brian Balyeat, who's on the faculty of Xavier's Williams College of Business and mentors the girls' volleyball team. "Sitting on the bench as an honorary coach, having a meal with players before the game, listening to their strategies—it's fun. I've seen the huge time commitment these student-athletes make to their sport. I see myself as another support mechanism for students to bridge the gap between being an athlete and being a student."

When the Stephen and Delores Smith Hall was being designed, Brian was on the planning committee for the new business education building with its scrolling stock tickers, high-tech classrooms and financial database terminals. "I thought it was significant that Father Graham asked us to make sure faculty offices and classrooms were inter-mixed," adding that the predictable result is more time with his students.

"Getting to know the students is part of what we do," says Thomas Hayes, chair and professor of marketing and college administration. "The culture at Xavier is student centered. One of the reasons we choose to teach here is the environment. Classes are small. We get to know everybody's name quickly. We want to see them."

Mentor for the men's basketball team, Tom goes to practices as well as games, watches videos with the team, meets with parents of recruits when they come to campus. He grew up on the west side of Cincinnati, went to my brother Tom's alma mater, St. Xavier High School, and graduated from Xavier University.

"I like the team anyway, have followed Xavier basketball forever. Mentors give the athletes another connection, someone else to talk to, someone else to trust with questions." He and his wife usually invite new freshmen over to their house for a meal when they arrive on campus. "Last year, we served edamame and guacamole," he said. "They said they'd never had it, but they tried it anyway."

I say that's two-fer—trust and a bigger culinary world.

Another more consequential foray into the "bigger world" took us to the nearby National Underground Railroad Freedom Center on Cincinnati's riverfront. Part of a diversity class I have been teaching for several years, the visit to the museum is on a Saturday, allowing me to schedule the rest of the day with speakers and discussions. That portion of the course, naturally, centers mostly on slavery and racial diversity, but the class also deals with issues of sexual orientation, ageism and sex discrimination.

Marian Weage, who started Cincinnati's chapter of PFLAG, an organization of parents, families and friends of people who are lesbian, gay, transgendered or bisexual, talked about the day her son told her he was gay. "It was a nightmare," she told the class. "I fell into a thousand pieces, cried for weeks. It was 1979, and people were so intolerant. I was afraid for him, afraid he would be hurt, afraid he would not be able to find a job. I was divorced from his father. I was afraid it was my fault. Afraid. Afraid. Afraid."

She didn't tell anybody at first. "When the kids come out, many parents go into the closet," she says. Her son started a support group in college and she went to some of the meetings. She also visited a mental health clinic, and "it was a great comfort to talk and learn." She brought a very warm perspective to the class.

Link Tague, who works at Children's Hospital in computer programming, talked about his anguish growing up. "I went to church every time the doors were open, sang in the choir. I thought the more I went to church, the better chance I could fix myself. I'm gay. I couldn't change myself. I tried. This is the way God made me." At the age of

18 he told his father, asking if he had suspected his son was gay. "Since you were a very little boy," his father answered. One clue, he told Link, was "when you joined Little League and didn't like anything about it but the outfit."

Attorney Louis Valencia, whose family came from Colombia, talked about cultural differences. "I tell them what it is to immigrate to this country, things that you leave behind, things you give up that make you who you are." His father, a surgeon, was unable to practice in this country until he could learn English and get a license. He wrangled permission to sit in the operating room of a hospital, where he spent every free moment with doctors and nurses, "listening to the lingo." According to Louis, "It took him five or six years. By the time he died he had no trace of an accent. People thought he was from Kentucky."

> ## As much as I could, I mimicked the coaches' use of multimedia, pictures, videos, diagrams.

Cliff Pope, a football coach and teacher at Elder High School, discussed growing up black and Catholic in Cincinnati. "I think this class creates a comfortable platform, a place where students can ask questions, even uncomfortable ones," he says.

We have lofty goals for this course—examining stereotyping and discrimination and their relation to economic and political power, increasing awareness of attitudes and behaviors and devising an action plan for students to be responsibly involved in cultural diversity issues. As much as I could, I mimicked the coaches' use of multimedia, pictures, videos, diagrams. Our workbook comes from the NCAA Champs Life Skills Program and includes simple language and conversation starters, such as:

"The thing I like about you is..."
"I was impressed when you said..."
"I identify with..."

Probably the most effective learning in this class takes place when the students begin talking with each other. I ask them to speak from their own experiences, respect the ideas and opinions of others and, at times, agree to disagree. Although we deal with sensitive issues, we do so in an atmosphere of respect. The course I teach for a one-hour credit is being phased out for the best possible reason.

Every major at Xavier now will offer a three-hour diversity class directly relevant to that course of study. For instance, the communications department offers Race,

Class, Gender and the Media, and education majors can sign up for Cultural Diversity in Education. An English major can study Literature and Moral Imagination: Marginalized Voices and Borderlands. Human Resources in a Diverse Society is part of the business curriculum, and history students can study the African American Struggle for Equality.

Reaching out beyond the campus borders and wrestling with complex human issues is an intentional part of the Xavier University learning experience. Visitors entering our campus are welcomed by a bronze statue of St. Francis Xavier wearing Japanese sandals with his Jesuit cassock. The priest is bestride steps replicating those at the Himeji castle outside Tokyo, and a plaque inscribed: "Patron of Xavier University and of foreign missions." Father Jim Hoff's charge to "prepare students intellectually, spiritually and morally to take their place in a rapidly changing global society and to work for the betterment of that society" has never been more urgent.

Our student-athletes are so very young, many of them with excruciatingly narrow life experience and completely tied up with their sport. I don't have a recipe for happiness and success for the rest of their lives, but part of my job while they are at this university is to make sure they are listening. I don't want to be the nun who raps them on the back on the head when they are not paying attention, but I desperately want them to learn the basic values in life and what they can contribute.

"Civilization is the encouragement of differences," according to Mohandus Gandhi.

Or, in the words of Brandon Cole, "Suddenly it's right in front of you. And you know."

The Spotlight and
the Point Guard

Bill Cosby, Father Hoff, and the alpha wolf.

Xavier University was making national news for all the right reasons, winning basketball games while keeping our eye on the ball academically. We Musketeers accepted our sudden fame with ill-disguised pride, sometimes wrapped in a mild joke. Maybe, somebody on campus might say, if they do enough stories about us on TV, they'll learn how to say our name. Egg-savier still occasionally fell off the tongues of even the best broadcasters.

No matter how they said it, the message was clear and exactly what we knew to be true. We had not lost our purpose in a quest to win basketball games.

Father Jim Hoff presented me with a special copy of the April 1993 *Reader's Digest*. There I was on page 187, "Sister and the Basketball Players." He'd had the magazine bound in Xavier Blue faux leather and he and Jeff Fogelson and Pete Gillen signed it, each in his own distinctive handwriting with sentiments that were special and dear to me. This team of three—just to push the analogy beyond tolerance—got the ball rolling, and I was gratified to be included. Jeff Fogelson called me the academic point guard. Later, Sean Miller nearly always introduced me to recruits and new players as "our point guard."

After years of rapt attention to Xavier's basketball players and their games and practices, I knew what this meant. I liked the mental image, and I hoped to live up to the responsibility. The point guard's job is to get teammates in the best position to score and play with a continual sense of the game clock, the score, and the remaining time-outs. The point guard plays on the perimeter to get the best view of the action. Oh, and point guard tends to be short.

The opening photo for the *Reader's Digest* story showed me awkwardly holding a ball, flanked by Brian Grant and Erik Edwards who, of course, towered over me. In case anybody missed the point, they called me diminutive and tiny, said the top of my head barely reached the numbers on their jerseys. I told the writer about Tyrone Hill and the overdue research paper and Derek Strong and the phone calls and Donnie. Erik Edwards was identified as a student who missed his final exams when he caught chicken pox. I set him up in the office next to mine during the Christmas break so I could help him study for makeup tests.

The story cited a 1991 nationwide survey by the *Chronicle of Higher Education*, which found that only 39 percent of men's basketball players earned degrees within five years. Our record then, as now, is 100 percent. Tom Eiser, Xavier University's sports media guru, grabbed hold of this asset and skillfully spread the word throughout the world of news directors, reporters and broadcast producers.

A 1984 Xavier grad, Tom has promoted XU basketball during twenty NCAA tournaments and has worked all but two of Xavier's 800-plus regular season and postseason men's basketball games since he was hired full-time in 1986. His men's basketball guide was voted "Best in the Nation" in 2011 by the College Sports Information Directors of America. More than any other single person, Tom is responsible for the message to the outside world of Xavier basketball's commitment to academics.

> A nun, an academic with an alphabet soup of degrees, anointed by a colorful and respected coach as an integral part of the team, I was a consistent message wrapped in Xavier blue.

Whenever I got a call from somebody asking for an interview, I always knew Tom had been behind it. And, although, some reporters may have mispronounced our name, I could tell by their questions that they were perched atop a mound of stats, reports and background from Tom. When I asked how he got such good media coverage for us, he said he conveyed to the media a consistent message of the presence of academics in the lives of the Xavier student-athletes.

Twenty-eight times a year, before and after every game, conference or non-conference, Tom's office publicizes student-athletes' academic majors, NCAA awards and academic awards. Whenever he has the opportunity, Tom steers reporters to study halls, meetings with tutors and on-the-road study sessions as well as practices and games. When he himself is interviewed, he almost always mentions his own pride in his Xavier University diploma. He puts writers in touch with athletes, then stands back and lets them talk.

In 1991, the Associated Press sent a story out to its hundreds of newspapers and television and radio stations around the country with the headline: All-Star Nun Keeps College Basketball Players on Academic Toes. That was the year Pete Gillen surprised me at the annual basketball awards presentation at a downtown Cincinnati hotel. I had offered the opening prayer, and then was startled to hear Coach Gillen mention a Most Valuable Player Award.

"We've never named an MVP," he said, "but there's one person we can't do without. We can lose a star forward or a great guard and still be competitive, but there's someone here who's irreplaceable." He held up a plaque, said my name and then all I could see was a crush of players and family and faculty. I will never forget that night. Tom, of course, made sure the word went out to all his media contacts.

After that, I think I was in every assignment editor's file. Pete was quoted in the *Los Angeles Times* about singling me out for this award, violating his own embargo against MVPs. "She's the one person we can't lose," he said. "There's an old saying that the strength of the wolf is in the pack, so we try to keep the pack more or less together rather than create alpha wolves and beta wolves."

I was an alpha wolf. I liked that. If I was going to be a walking, talking figure of speech and cliché—a simile and metaphor for every sports-writing occasion, I preferred this to "bone-white hair, thin as a rake, sharp as a razor."

I got even more requests for interviews, and I understood clearly my value to our image. A nun, an academic with an alphabet soup of degrees, anointed by a colorful and respected coach as an integral part of the team, I was a consistent message wrapped in Xavier blue. Truthfully, it made me a little nervous. At first, it was just phone interviews, asking for comment. Then, I was sitting down with reporters. I kept my focus on the one thing I felt qualified to discuss—academics—trying to gently lead them from their fascination with, as ABC News put it, "At five-foot-four inches tall, a towering figure of inspiration and determination."

Good heavens.

I told ABC's Ron Claiborne: "If they have played for Xavier for four years, we have been successful in getting them through the degree program. They deserve the credit for that. All I have to do is, to some extent, guide them."

Tom Eiser's advice, and my own instincts, helped me avoid comparing our record to other schools and voicing opinions on issues unrelated to what I do with our own athletes. Consistency. Focus. "Athletes must fulfill all the academic requirements if they want to play ball," I said over and over to reporters, easy to do because it was the same message I gave to athletes:

"If you don't fulfill those requirements, we're not going to do any fudging. You are not going to play basketball."

Jeff Fogelson told me to relax and just continue to say what I believe, just say it honestly. So I did. I tried to engage reporters in the athletes' accomplishments and the university's support. When *The New York Times* reporter asked me to meet with him over coffee during a tournament in Atlantic City and asked me about our graduation rate, I emphasized our long-standing commitment to academics: "Our alumni over

Keeping our purpose—Jason Love, Andrew Taylor and Jamel McLean.

the years have told me they're so proud of the graduation rate." I told him about study tables and tutors.

"My job is to make sure we don't waste their opportunity to also get a degree," I told a Fox News reporter, who invited me to share "some of the craziest excuses" I've gotten from students who missed class. "They are pretty level with me," I said truthfully, adding that I always tell them to call faculty to, "do the right thing."

When *Wall Street Journal* reporter Mark Yost asked about our graduation rate and practices, I said, "They may have been attracted to Xavier by a coach, but from the very start we make it clear that they are here to receive an education. We place a great deal of emphasis on educating the individual. That's very much a Christian ideal." Mr. Yost is author of the book, *Varsity Green: A Behind the Scenes Look at Culture and Corruption in College Athletics*. He took the time to explain our curriculum and called me "feisty," reporting that Xavier makes sure basketball players spend as much time in class as they do in the gym.

Another important point Tom Eiser stressed is that it is not enough to tell the media about a student-athlete's academic progress, it is important to demonstrate the changes in the athlete as he expresses himself. Tom takes time to work with the athletes, teaching them to make eye contact, speak in well-formed sentences that are grammatically correct and clarify their thoughts. His advice always is to speak respectfully of past and present opponents. Besides encouraging them to talk to reporters, he puts them at the microphone in the media room at the Cintas Center.

Most of the time, this works. One time, it went horribly wrong.

Since 1927, the University of Cincinnati Bearcats and the Xavier Musketeers have squared off against each other on the basketball court. Off-again, on-again for several years, since 1946 the Crosstown Shootout, as it came to be called, became one of the hottest tickets in town. In 1990, a Cincinnati TV station refused to interrupt their coverage of the game for the State of the Union Address. Xavier Athletics Director Greg Christopher says watching the game on television while he was a student at Miami was "my introduction to Xavier."

In the immediate years leading up to a brawl on the court in December of 2011, there were technical fouls and heated insults at the Xavier-UC games, as well as trash talk on the radio and in barbershops, clubs and dormitories. Imagine if Michigan and Ohio State were located three miles apart in the same city. Social media was aglow with, at times, provocative and ugly tweets and blogs.

I was in my usual seat in the Cintas Center stands that night, watching the game that was close at first with eight ties and six lead changes in the first half, but Xavier led 34–25 at halftime. With 18.6 seconds remaining, Tu Holloway scored on a layup to give the Musketeers a 76–53 lead. At the two-minute mark, I had eased out of my seat, as I usually do, to go back to the locker room to greet players as they come off the floor. I waited. And waited.

Out on the floor, there was a free-for-all. Officials stopped the game with 9.4 seconds left to go. I was shocked to see Kenny Frease coming toward me, dazed, with blood on his cheek. Back in the media room, Tu Holloway and Mark Lyons were taking questions from reporters, just as all our players have been encouraged to do for years.

"It's pretty standard," Tom Eiser says. "The stars of the game step forward and talk." This is not without careful preparation. Players regularly practice simulated press conferences and stand-ups. Coaches, outside speakers such as Clark Kellogg from CBS Sports and other experts reinforce the lessons: Articulate carefully. Look the questioner in the eye. Speak in complete sentences. Remember the message. Think about your answer.

"They've done a great job over the years. Media interviews are good training for a lot of things in life," Tom says, including job interviews.

But that night, it was, in Tom's words, "a perfect storm."

Still in uniform and no doubt with adrenalin still coursing though his veins, Xavier's point guard Tu Holloway said, "We've got a whole bunch of gangsters in the locker room—not thugs, but tough guys on the court." Tu added, "In a few days, everyone will forget."

Immediately afterward, Coach Chris Mack came to the microphone and spoke with his customary professional cool. He said he and the University of Cincinnati Coach Mick Cronin have been friends since the fifth grade and that the young men who spoke just before him were "good kids" with "big hearts." He drew the focus back to basketball.

President Michael Graham tried that night for historical perspective, "Our basketball program is expected to, and has for so many years now, represented the highest ideals of sportsmanship and ethical conduct." Coach Mack tweeted, "If my players say they've been taught to be tough their whole life, they mean ON THE FLOOR. Nothing else is condoned."

But it wasn't over.

The lurid reference to gangsters and thugs was discussed in broadcast, print and on the internet with great solemnity as if nobody had ever heard of a kill shot in volleyball or Babe Ruth and Murderers' Row. Hands were wrung. Sides were taken. Everybody from the presidents on down to the players from both universities apologized. Many times. Videos of the thirty-second melee were on a seemingly endless loop on television and available 24/7 on YouTube. Players were suspended amid muttering that the incident was being blown out of proportion. Two proud institutions were bruised. Fans were by turns angry and ashamed. So, we did what academics do. We looked for the teachable moment. We sought perspective.

Dr. John Getz from Xavier's English department organized a plan with University of Cincinnati English professor Beverly Brannan. After focus groups with students, including student-athletes, they offered a joint course, Literature and Moral Imagination. Students enrolled from both universities and alternated meeting on each campus. "We didn't address the fight directly, John says. "We worked on larger issues of leadership and community." Speakers included coaches and community leaders, such as former Cincinnati mayor Roxanne Qualls.

"She was especially good," John says. "Got the group talking about leadership and the role of athletics and athletes in the community." One of the students asked how they could get involved. Cincinnati has fifty-two neighborhoods, Roxanne told them. Start there. The professors divided the class into smaller groups including students from each university for presentations and projects.

The teachable moment extended to everybody. As Kenny Frease's mother, Marge, who played college basketball for Youngstown State in the 1980s, told an ESPN reporter, "That much anger in your soul is not a good thing." The next year, both schools held a joint press conference at the National Underground Freedom Center, announcing that the game would now be called the "Skyline Chili Crosstown Classic." Students from both schools wore Crosstown Classic tee-shirts imprinted with both the Bearcat and the Musketeer logos on a community walk to celebrate diversity. For the next two years, the game was held at the U.S. Bank Arena.

Back on campus, Carol Maas, an administrative assistant at the front desk in the Cintas Center's sports offices, was getting a terrible dose of perspective. Breast cancer. A particularly virulent form. Everybody was concerned, but Tu Holloway was the person who went to the hospital during her treatments. "He called me every day, even on the days of his games," Carol says. Tom Eiser gave Tu a small stash of bobble heads for his family. Tu gave one to Carol. "He has a really good heart," she says, echoing Chris Mack's just-after-the-brawl sentiments.

"People reach conclusions in 140 characters and on talk radio, often before they have any facts," Tom Eiser says. "It was a learning experience for everyone. We'll be okay as long as we stay who we are. I am proud of what Xavier stands for." He continues to put student-athletes at the microphone and at the center of press conferences. This is not simply about games. It's about the life they will confront after college.

John Getz has been working on improvements to the English 205 course, Literature and Moral Imagination. Every one of our senior basketball players received a diploma last year. Carol Maas is back at her desk. After being named to the 2011–12 National All-Jesuit Men's Basketball Team, Tu Holloway played basketball in Turkey and Belgium. He's back in town, and we talk frequently. Isn't my fellow point guard better defined by his work in the classroom and his compassion for a sick friend than his time on the basketball court and his seconds before a microphone?

Xavier and the University of Cincinnati announced in May of 2014 that they've agreed to continue the annual rivalry for at least ten more years, bringing the games back to the campuses. Coach Mack said it will be called the Shootout, "which is what everybody called it anyway." Greg Christopher said it's "an opportunity to re-set this great rivalry in a positive light."

So, are we whistling in the wind with marches and get-together classes and tutorials for public communication? Is it window dressing? Of course it's not. How could I think otherwise? I come from a religious order of women who risked their lives to teach.

A trip to the Bahamas. Basketball lessons for inner-city children. A mother's story about her gay son. Study tables and tutors. A class at the Freedom Center. A theater production about the black experience in America. Skip Prosser's "Academics First" poster. Father Graham's steady support for discourse and outreach. These things are intrinsic, threads in the fabric of this institution. My life's work has at its heart a belief that education is the answer to life's most difficult questions and that our good God loves all of us and will bless our every attempt to be better human beings.

Xavier University will remain in the spotlight, which we have learned sometimes sheds more heat than light. But our message is clear and exactly what we know to be true. We have not lost our purpose in a quest to win basketball games.

18

Chris Mack and The Picture Window

Coach Mack, a career that turned on a knee.

On a warmish spring Saturday, the parking lot and sidewalk on the east side of Cintas Center blooms with color. Girls in impossibly short skirts and dangerous shoes and young men in shirtsleeves self consciously tugging neckties push open the glass doors to the Schiff Conference Center. Older women in bright scarves and dressy pantsuits and men in more somber suits, wearing neckties that appear less temporary, climb out of their mostly made-in-America Hondas and Fords and Chevrolets and move down the steps, headed in the same direction.

The Scholar-Athlete Awards have come a long way since Father Hoff handed me twenty-five instructions scribbled on yellow legal paper, notes about how to improve it. I think he would be pleased.

The pianist plays the feather theme from Forrest Gump as Bobbie Terlau from the Academic Advising Center carefully lines up trophies and certificates. There's a chart telling everybody where to sit, where to stand, where to enter, where to exit. Academic adviser Chris Barbour hands out programs to parents, faculty and friends with a broad smile that looks as if he uses every muscle in his face and a couple in his shoulders. Father John LaRocca, S.J., professor of history and long-time friend of student-athletes, gives the invocation, his diamond-patterned sweater vest a warm note with his clerical collar.

Kimberly Powers Hoyt, another academic adviser and mistress of ceremonies, asks that we hold our applause. Nobody does. She grins and rescinds the order. It still astonishes me when I look around and realize how many athletes we serve—about 300 right now in eighteen men and women's sports. Besides Kim and Chris, our student-athletes are advised by Erik Alanson and tutored by about a dozen professionals.

Erik is on stage with several others, including our president, Father Graham, implicit evidence of the importance the university places on this day. Dr. John Kucia, administrative vice president whose title really should read Chancellor in Charge of Everything Running Smoothly, also is seated on the dais. John is the one who first came to me, gently suggesting we should make plans about the future of academic advising for Xavier's athletes.

I knew what he meant. Me.

It was in 2008. We need to think about your retirement, John said. Well, I could hardly feign shock. *What? Retirement? Me? I'm only 76. Just getting started. In the prime of my life. Race you to the the D'Artagnan statue. Want to arm wrestle?*

Of course, I didn't say any of these things.

I told John that I didn't want to impose, that I realized at some point this would happen. I had seen plenty of my sisters who suddenly couldn't remember what they'd had for breakfast. If this happens to me, I told John, just call the Provincial House in Reading and they'll yank me out. I said, "Yes, let's think about it. That would be a good idea."

John was straightforward, kind and skillful. I remembered how insistent Xavier's board of trustees had been with Father Hoff, almost from the moment he arrived on campus, about planning for the day when somebody else would pick up the reins.

> **I could feel this new job growing around me.**

Truly, I was not dismayed. Around that time, Oprah announced that she was leaving her show, so I couldn't help thinking I was in good company.

And God has always let me know where I was needed next.

In September of 2009, Mike Bobinski offered me the job of NCAA Division I faculty athletics representative for Xavier when Dr. David Hellkamp of the psychology department retired. He suggested hiring additional academic advisers for the day-to-day work and beginning to train an eventual successor. You don't have to dream up a job for me, I said. I can practice law, I can teach, I can...

John didn't let me finish, as I remember.

We want you here, he said. There's plenty to do. I consulted with institutions which have made similar transitions and found some of the best advice close to home. Sister Fran Repka, a Sister of Mercy in Cincinnati, was insightful and pragmatic. A psychologist, she headed up the Archdiocese's Consultation Services for Religious and Clergy and founded Mercy Professional Services. I followed her advice, taking care not to step back too abruptly. At meetings including the entire advisory staff, we'd discuss specific problems and brainstorm solutions. It allowed us to appreciate our strengths as a team and let me see who needed my help most urgently.

John was right. There was always plenty to do, and I could feel this new job growing around me. Recruiting for men's basketball is increasingly competitive, and these are the athletes who most often arrive on campus with a gap between what they know and what they need to know.

Xavier University's Graduation Success Rate (GSR) for all teams, as defined and tracked by the NCAA, is 97 percent, twelfth in the nation and first in the Big East conference. Ten current Xavier teams posted a GSR rate of 100 percent: men's basketball, men's golf, men's swimming, men's tennis, men's track, women's soccer, women's swimming, women's tennis, women's track and women's volleyball. Xavier's baseball team was ranked next-highest at 95 percent.

So there really is plenty to celebrate at our annual honors program, and plenty to do to maintain our record.

My title now is Special Assistant to the President/NCAA Faculty Athletics Representative. Besides continuing to work with the academic advising staff, I help with fund-raising and public awareness. Replacing me with somebody else willing to live in the midst of the students, be on call 24/7 and compensated just enough to cover modest expenses was never considered likely. Since our initial conversations in 2008, an endowment fund for academic services for athletes has been established, and the university made a commitment to continue the services and policies that put our student-athletes in the top echelon of collegiate achievement.

Hewing to NCAA requirements is increasingly complex, and my law degree is helpful in sorting out the rules. I've had time to start new programs, such as the faculty mentors, and have been exploring software and electronics that might help student-athletes recover their classes real-time while they're immersed in seasonal competition, including road trips. It is a far cry from the early days with Doris Jackson when my office in Alter Hall looked like a supply closet, filled with supplies nobody wanted, and Jeff Fogelson pointed me directly at the basketball players.

Flanked by a great team (from left), Tom Eiser, John Kucia, Bill Daily, and Pete Gillen at the 1992 *Cincinnati Enquirer* Women of the Year Awards.

A player well worth the risk to Pete Gillen's car—Jamal Walker with his wife, Aiesha, and children, Nina and Jamal.

To mixed reviews, the coaches told them I was now their full-time adviser. There might have been a little "sticker shock" at the beginning, for recruits who believed that "their" academic athletics adviser's job was simply to fix things so they could show up to play ball—find them easy classes and grease the skids with their professors. From the beginning, I knew my assignment was more difficult and more wonderful.

I started talking with the players about planning for a time when basketball would no longer be in their lives. What are you going to do, I asked them, after basketball? Not just for the rest of your time at Xavier, but for the fifty or sixty years after that. I remember the day I dragged Jamal Walker into the World Without Basketball, if not kicking and screaming, certainly sweating and grousing. Pete Gillen, who recruited him in 1987 from the Bronx, said Jamal had swagger and used to tell stories about finding him in a neighborhood that was so tough the coach was surprised to find his car still there with all its tires when he left.

I'd say Jamal proved to be worth the risk to Pete's ride.

He was the point guard who led the team to our first-ever Sweet 16 in 1990. A four-year starter, Jamal was quick and made dramatic shots and passes, often in mid-air. He was fun to watch. But he was no fun at all when I insisted that he keep an appointment to interview for an internship with an accounting firm. I tracked him down that morning, and sent him over to the career center where they tuned him up—helped him with a resume and gave him some advice on interviewing and how to dress.

My advice was, as usual, "Listen to what they tell you. Leave street smarts at the door." I offered to drive him in my nice little Chevy Nova, which didn't have much leg room. Jamal was cramped and griped all the way downtown because I didn't have air conditioning. When we arrived, he was dripping wet and in a terrible mood. "This is so dumb." We took an elevator to the top of one of Cincinnati's tallest buildings. The elevator doors opened on a panoramic view. We could see from Coney Island almost down to Indiana.

Clearly impressed, Jamal said, "This is different from what I expected."

Exactly the point. He won the job, and his mentor there helped him set up a bank account—his first—and learn how to manage his salary. "I liked the money," he says, "but I sure didn't like sitting behind a desk all day." Part of my pep talk about jobs and internships was also to "get to know what makes you feel, happy, successful, enthusiastic." If you love basketball above all other things, I would tell athletes, maybe it can be part of your life, even if you don't play.

Coach and athletics director for fourteen years at Woodward High School in the Bond Hill neighborhood of Cincinnati, Jamal now is a substitute teacher at Princeton High School in a suburb northeast of there.

"When I was a kid," Jamal says, "basketball kept me out of trouble. In my neighborhood, there were gangs and drugs and hustlers. I stayed away from all that because I was bouncing a ball." Growing up with a single mother, he says, "my family life was stable, but it took a village to raise this child. I had a lot of support from people in the neighborhood and in school."

Maybe that "village" was good practice for him when he came to Xavier. A B-student in high school, he admits "everything was a lot harder when I got to college." But Jamal took advantage of the help we had to offer, worked with tutors, improved his study skills and became lots better at managing his time. After graduation and playing overseas for several seasons, he returned to Cincinnati with his wife, Aiesha, and two children, Nina and Jamal.

At Woodward, Jamal says he "tried to duplicate for my students what I experienced at Xavier—academic advisers, study halls." He says he wishes he could have hired somebody for his students "who would have knocked on their doors and been their alarm clock."

I think he might have meant me.

Much has been made of the 129 rings of Derek Strong's phone. Lenny Brown would say later that he longed for the days of ignoring those simple phone calls. According to Lenny, when the athletes bought answering machines, they could expect "long, really long messages" from me. "I would groan and put my pillow over my head," Lenny said, "but it would just go on and on. You might as well just get up and go to class."

Permission to put the nun's habit in mothballs was, to me, permission to use everything the modern world has to offer to my students. I have progressed from answering machines to voice mail to instant messaging. I am investigating video streaming of lectures, new electronic devices and software, as well as post-graduate assistance for athletes.

As Father Mike Graham says, "Our challenge is to use this technology, alongside caring professors."

My work at Xavier is not about a piece of paper. A diploma. It never has been. This is about the rest of their lives. A new Gallup-Purdue Index Report, a survey of 30,000 American college graduates on issues of employment, job engagement and well being, found that the collegians who thrive in later life are the ones who take something away from their years at the institution besides their degree. If, during those college years, they had emotional support, professors who "made me excited about learning," "cared about me as a person" or "encouraged my hopes and dreams," the survey showed they had double the odds of finding success at work and three times the odds of general well-being.

Jamal's teammate, Jamie Gladden, remembers choosing Xavier amid an "overwhelming" series of calls from Oklahoma State, Tulsa University, the University of Cincinnati, Ohio State and Drake University. "It almost felt like I was more of a number than a person," he says. "But every time I talked to a Xavier coach, it was a totally different experience. They didn't promise anything they couldn't deliver."

Jamie said Skip Prosser, then an assistant coach, warned him, "Whatever you get here, you're going to have to earn it." I suspect when they are listening to a coach, even one like Skip who peppered his conversation with quotes from great philosophers, they assume that the total discussion is about athletics. It was up to me to break the news to them that we expected more of them than a flashy jump shot. Jamie, who went to work for a financial firm in Atlanta after graduation in 1993, says he respected the idea of earning his place and also liked Xavier's high graduation rate.

One of the hardest concepts for these young athletes with talent and swagger is the notion that they should see books as a hedge against the day when, as Pete Gillen used to say, "the air goes out of the basketball." What if, I would ask them carefully, you get hurt?

Xavier's head coach Chris Mack, a steadfastly vocal supporter of academics, is a dramatic example of a basketball career that turned on a knee. A 1992 Xavier graduate who grew up in North College Hill, Chris was a two-time team captain as a player for Xavier under Pete Gillen after transferring from the University of Evansville in Indiana. He sat out for a year to comply with NCAA rules, then during play for the Musketeers blew out his knees, one at a time.

Everybody says he rehabbed like crazy, which I don't doubt. Chris has enormous grit and self-discipline. He played his senior year, but never more than about five minutes a game. After graduation, he signed with a European team, but "my knees brought me back home," he says. "I thought maybe it was not in God's plan for me to continue to play basketball. The handwriting was on the wall, but, man, it was hard to focus on those words."

His sister, Carrie, was playing senior guard at McAuley High School, which had lost its junior varsity coach. When the varsity coach, who was doing double duty, heard that Carrie's brother was back, he hired Chris. "I loved it, loved being part of the game again." Two years later, he took a job as head coach at another all-girls Cincinnati high school, Mt. Notre Dame, where he rallied the fans as well as the team, installing couches for spectators on the stage next to the playing floor, ordering pizzas for halftime and passing out fliers for the "Rage on the Stage."

He came back to Xavier as Director of Basketball Operations from 1999 to 2001, then spent three seasons as an assistant coach at Wake Forest with Skip Prosser, returning to Xavier again in 2004 as an assistant under Sean Miller. When Sean left for Arizona in 2009, Chris was ready. "Some coaches like to have specialists on their staff," Chris says, "one assistant who recruits, one who scouts. Skip wanted each coach on his staff to think and act like a head coach. That was such a gift. It made me well-rounded."

Rumors of his leaving Xavier University swirl around him regularly. But I hope he will decide that God wants him here for a while longer. "The Big East ratchets up our exposure," Chris says. "We all feel a pressure to succeed. Basketball is the window to our university. We want this window to just keep getting bigger and bigger."

Coach Mack's boss, Director of Athletics Greg Christopher, calls basketball "the front porch." But however they describe the sport, both have been unwavering champions of academics. Coach Mack says during the recruiting process, "My number one consideration is how that person will fit with Xavier, the university. We want them to succeed academically."

And that is the key.

Study halls, meeting with athletes, tutors, the best intentions in the world—none of this will turn out successful student-athletes without the right structure in place and without support from the top, people who see these young men as more than entertainers who bring money and cheers to the institution.

It meant the world to me when Father Graham told me to do "whatever is necessary" to help our illiterate basketball player Jimmy learn to read while he was at the university, even if he wasn't playing well, even if he wasn't playing at all. And after the fracas during the 2011 Crosstown Shootout, Father Graham pushed his way through the hallway to the locker room with one question, and it was not "How is this going to play on TV?" He demanded to know: "How is Kenny's eye?"

The Jesuit Cura Personalis, serving and caring for the whole person, which drew me to the university nearly three decades ago, has been at the heart of my assignment. "Your duty is to the student, not the team," Jeff Fogelson said then. That is still the guiding principle, improved by what we've learned from our athletes, from coaches and faculty. From my first conversations with John Kucia, I was confident the time-tested policies would help serve the people trustee Bob Kohlhepp rightfully calls both the customer and the product.

This is my best summary of the basics that have worked for us:

Academic support and life skills for athletes should be done by an independent office that has status within the university, at arm's length from the athletics department. If a coach who recruited an athlete and organized a $50,000 to $60,000 twelve-month scholarship demands extra hours from the student, it's hard for him to say no. An independent advising office for the student-athletes can intercede—working with coaches, faculty and administrators to find balance. The end game is always a successful student. Academic advising is team specific. Besides knowing how to accommodate the obvious differences in each sport's season in the academic sequence, each team has its own culture. Players are most likely to respond to someone who understands the sport they play and who has established a working relationship with their coaches, as well as their teachers. The center must be staffed by people professionally prepared and educated to be advisers. Adult tutors, who have good grasp on a variety of disciplines, are essential, as are student tutors who can perform less complex tasks, such as filling in a basketball player on what he missed when the team was away for a game. Everybody must resist the impulse to do the work for the student-athlete.

Study habits should be established early. Every freshman student-athlete at Xavier is required to be at study tables for two hours a day, Sunday through Thursday, every week of their first semester, whether in or out of season. After the first semester, freshmen who have earned less than a 3.0 GPA are required to continue study tables. For the rest of their Xavier career, any student athlete who falls under a 3.0 GPA will be required to attend weekly study tables. The program needs a physical infrastructure, including a resource center where student athletes can study and have access to computers, printers and, of course, their advisers and tutors. The best hope for success in dealing with student-athletes is to forge a relationship and that means spending time with them outside the formal academic and advising offices and study tables—attending practices and games, traveling with the team, getting to know the student-athlete's support system, family, friends, roommates. Chris Mack will—for a long time, I hope—bring us students who can play Front Porch-Picture Window basketball for Xavier University. Once they get here, they will find, as Jamie did, that we deliver on our promises. They also will find allies they might not expect— people who will help them prepare for a life without basketball. Or soccer or swimming. Or any sport at all.

The breadth of responsibility and expectation is reflected in the awards made to these young people on Honors Day in the spring—laurels for service, for grades, for character. Some trophies bear the names of alumni, who continue to involve themselves in their alma mater, who would not accept nor support the idea of an athletics program that wins games and loses academic and spiritual purpose. The culture and the foundation are strong. When it comes time for me to step back from my life's work—more firmly and more finally—I do not worry for the future. Not at all.

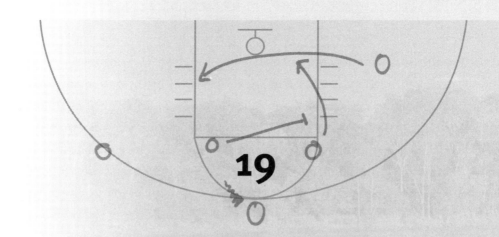

19

All for One and the Launching Pad

Victor Fleming accepts the Blackburn McCafferty MVP
Award from Tom Siemers, a staunch team supporter.

$\mathcal{A}$ small, shadowy figure moved quietly through the plane. The hour was late, and Xavier's basketball team was flying back to Cincinnati after a tough loss. Genny Sedler was dispensing homemade chocolate brownies from a Tupperware container. In my opinion, it helped.

Coach Gillen used to tell his players that the thousands who attend games love you when you win. When you lose, only Siemers, Sedler and Conaton will care about you. He was talking about the late Tom Siemers, retired chairman of Franklin Savings, who graduated from Xavier in 1953, Tom Sedler, former CEO of Home City Ice, a 1951 Xavier alumni, and Michael Conaton, retired vice-chairman of the Midland Co. and a 1955 Xavier University graduate, who has served not only as chairman of the university's board of trustees but as our interim president.

These three men have indeed cared for the university and its students with remarkable loyalty and generosity, paying the university the greatest tribute of all—sending their children and grandchildren to us to be educated. Each has put his stamp on the campus and each is responsible for nudging us forward with treasure, time and good sense. The fourth floor of Cintas Center, home to the Athletics Offices, is named in honor of Tom Siemers. My office is located in the building bearing Mike Conaton's name. The Sedler Family Center for Entrepreneurship was opened in 2010.

It is typical that Tom Sedler not only comes to the games, but he gets up early in the morning beforehand to bake pastry for them as well. He guesses he has been doing this for roughly three decades. "Dad died when I was 10," he says. "I went to work, then to night school. I've always appreciated someone who is willing to work hard. And these kids work hard."

Years ago, before the university's prodigious array of fitness equipment, Tom Sedler hired basketball players during the summer to stack bags of ice on skids. "Ice is pretty heavy," Tom says. "The coaches loved it. The boys really bulked up."

I truly don't think our academic advising program could have survived those first few years without Genny and Tom. We had no money. Pete Gillen and I used to meet with the Sedlers for lunch. Pete would bring Xavier sweatshirts or banners for them, and I would bring a list of things we needed to keep the kids eligible—money for tutors, sometimes even supplies. Tom would write a check.

They'd wave off thanks and instead spend time telling us about the latest exploits of basketball players who'd visited their Indiana farm or about their own four sons, all of whom attended Xavier.

Tom Siemers, too, spent time with Xavier athletes off the court, mentoring them and getting to know their families. "It's hard for me to make comparisons," Tom said once, "because my life has been with Xavier, but it seems like something special to me. There's a camaraderie among students, faculty and staff that I haven't seen anyplace else."

Maybe Father Finn had the right idea. No tigers, bulldogs, eagles or mules for the Xavier fans. Our mascot is a Musketeer, the noble D'Artagnan from Alexandre Dumas' novel, *The Three Musketeers*. Father Francis J. Finn, a Jesuit and member of the Xavier University board of trustees for many years until his death in 1928, proposed the name Musketeers in 1925 to promote chivalry and recognize Xavier's ties with French culture.

French speaking young men from Louisiana were among the first students at Xavier in the 1830s, and the first Jesuit priest of Xavier, in 1840, was father John Anthony Elet, a native of the French speaking provinces in Belgium. The great patron of Xavier University, St. Francis Xavier, a native of Spain, received his university education at the College of St. Barbe at the University of Paris and helped found the Jesuit Order in Paris in 1540. So, Father Finn reasoned, the Musketeer, a dedicated guard of the King of France, was a fine symbol of the "All for One, One for All" spirit.

Cintas Center's dedication in 2000 included the unveiling of a new statue of D'Artagnan replacing a battered version, which had stood on campus since 1968. Roland Moore, a 1935 alumnus, donated the money to honor his French wife, and Tom Tsuchiya, who created the statues on campus of St. Francis Xavier and Father Jim Hoff, was commissioned. Mr. Tsuchiya also created the life-sized bronze statues at the gates of the Great American Ball Park and the fifty-two-foot tall statue of Jesus at the Solid Rock Church in Monroe, a landmark along Interstate 75 to the east.

> **If anybody embodies the Xavier spirit at its best, it would be Michael Conaton.**

Our eight-and-a-half-foot tall bronze D'Artagnan is a landmark as well, just outside the Cintas Center's main entrance. The hilt on his sword depicts a basketball.

"All for one and one for all," Tom Siemers said. "That sounds about right." Right up until his death in the spring of 2014, Tom stayed in touch with his own classmates, as well as players he met over the years, including Tyrone Hill and Michael Davenport.

"Tyrone says Michael and I are two people he can count on because, he said, 'You two don't want anything from me.'"

Indeed, the three men Pete Gillen so accurately described have been givers, not takers. And if anybody embodies the Xavier spirit at its best, it would be Michael Conaton. Mike and I have been friends for years, and I see him often as we both serve on the Athenaeum and Mount Notre Dame Advisory boards. A 1955 XU graduate, he played football and was "horribly disappointed when the football program was scrapped." He was a trustee at the time. "I made a big pitch. The Jesuits made a motion. And it was gone."

Football went, but Mike stayed. "When I got out of the Marines, I wanted a mission. My mission then, as now, is to be a person for others who doesn't give in to himself. Every night before I go to bed, I reflect on my mission." His goal, he says, is to be principled and not step outside the path he has set for himself, to "treat others as you want to be treated, in life, in business, all the time." I have never known him to deviate from these principles.

He calls the Jesuits a "tremendous influence" on his life. In fact, he nearly became a priest after the death of his first wife, Margie, a friend of mine from The Summit. She died after a long struggle with lupus. Their children were grown, and Mike was lonesome and distraught. Father Hoff was a great friend to him at that time. "He was my brother," Mike says simply.

Three years later, he met his current wife, Nancy, and shelved the idea of the priesthood. The closest he ever came was when he was acting president of Xavier after Father DiUlio left in 1990. By charter, the Jesuit colleges are to be led by a Jesuit priest. Fordham University President Joseph O'Hare chaired the Association of Jesuit Colleges and Universities annual meeting. The twenty-eight college presidents—twenty-seven of them Jesuit priests—ringed the table. "Conaton," Father O'Hare said with mock severity, "if you're going to sit here you have to turn your collar around."

While he was, in effect, CEO of Xavier University, he continued as CEO of the Midland company, a multimillion-dollar specialty insurance company with 1,500 employees. "I had excellent vice presidents," he says modestly. "My one big decision at Xavier was when the BASF plant exploded next to campus." One of his excellent vice presidents, Xavier's John Kucia, notified Mike Conaton. "I said dramatically: Evacuate the campus."

John replied, "I already did."

The site of the chemical manufacturing plant was deeded to the university in 2000 and, combined with the old Zumbiel Packaging Plant acreage, is bringing new life to the corner of Dana Avenue and Montgomery Road as University Station. The demolition work included massive recycling—32,365 tons of concrete, 1,520 tons of brick, 205 tons of asphalt and 2,679 tons of steel. In addition, the university salvaged materials from the houses along Dana and Ledgewood avenues that were demolished to make way for the projects.

The "greening" of our campus continued during construction of the new Learning Commons, recognized by the U.S. Green Building Council for its environmentally friendly materials and energy efficient heating and cooling systems. When it came time to name the massive new structure, longtime Xavier benefactor Charles P. Gallagher was offered the honor. He requested that it be called the Michael J. Conaton Learning Commons. "It was a simple decision," Charlie said when the building plan was announced in 2009. "Mike Conaton and Father Hoff had a vision for moving Xavier forward, a vision that we are seeing come true today."

That vision has been substantially supported by Charles Gallagher, a Toledo native and 1960 Xavier graduate and emeritus trustee. Chairman of the Denver-based private equity firm that bears his name, he seems never to forget his Midwest roots. His $9 million matching gift helped build our $18 million Gallagher Student Center in 2002, and he also underwrites the education of inner-city students from his alma maters, St. Martin de Porres and Central Catholic High School in Toledo.

"When you get right down to it," says Father Mike Graham, "Charlie's shoulders are some of the shoulders upon which the future of Xavier University is being built." Massive projects with long reaching effects, for sure, but I have always been touched by the tiny pub in Gallagher Center named for Stephen Ryan, Charlie's college roommate who passed away in 1981.

And I think when he insisted on putting Mike's name on the Learning Commons—such a fundamental part of the Hoff Academic Quad—the wise and generous man was honoring another significant Xavier friendship.

I know Mike is just kidding when he says he missed his one big decision when BASF exploded. I think his biggest and best decision was not to take no for an answer from Father Hoff when he declined to interview for the Xavier presidency. Besides the bricks and mortar growth, the two men worked together to build a skein of fifty alumni chapters around the country, creating a national association and energizing more than 60,000 Xavier graduates across the nation and strengthening their bonds to Xavier University. When the team plays in one of these cities, or nearby, it is amazing to me the level of support they bring to the team.

*D*espite the fact that the Big East conference means that away games are really away, we always have a healthy contingent of Cincinnati folks. Greg Ionna charters a bus once a year and brings his entire family. Last year about two dozen of them skated through the icy roads for ten hours to cheer us on at the Marquette game in Milwaukee.

"We were covered for all situations," Greg jokes. "We had three doctors, five nurses and a Roman Catholic priest on board. He sprinkled the tires with holy water, and after we saw all the cars that slid off the road, we decided it must have worked." CEO of the C.M. Paula company, Greg serves on the Athenaeum and Sisters of Notre Dame boards with Mike Conaton and me, and Mike and Greg chaired a capital campaign for the Athenaeum in 2011 that raised $20 million.

Greg, who worked his way through Xavier with a series of jobs at Kroger, says, "Going to basketball games was one of the few college experiences I had." After graduation in 1963, he kept going to games, sitting on bleachers in Schmidt Field House, watching "some of the worst basketball you ever wanted to watch. It has been fun to see the program grow. Walking into Cintas Center, well, I just love it."

The continued development at Xavier, he says, is a typically Jesuit lesson: patience, dedication, discipline. "Then you go out into the world and use what you've learned," he says. And the second part of that, he says, is "to give back."

Tom Siemers said, "What you got at Xavier from the Jesuits, pure and simple, was attention to character, the whole man." He and his wife, Susie, not only bought season tickets for men's home basketball games and several of the out-of-town games, but they've traveled to colleges around the country, visiting former coaches and assistants such as Pete Gillen, Jeff Battle, Mark Schmidt and Dino Gaudio.

Many Xavier alums keep up with the team during the season with a shorter trip to the Dilly Deli in the Mariemont Strand, east of Cincinnati on Wooster Pike, for a weekly live radio broadcast. Head Coach Chris Mack is flanked on a raised platform by Xavier Hall of Fame former players, Joe Sunderman and Byron Larkin, who field polite questions from the phone-in 55 KRC audience and the folks in the Dilly. Byron and

Joe are pros who keep things moving, and Chris is smooth and congenial. He gets a lot of strategy advice, which he accepts graciously.

Joe, who graduated from Xavier in 1979, not only is part of the radio broadcasts but volunteers for countless fund-raisers and banquets. In his senior season, before he was sidelined by an injury, Joe helped XU capture what is still regarded as the most prestigious regular season men's basketball championship in school history, beating nationally ranked Southern Cal and host Tennessee to win the Volunteer Classic. Joe had 19 points and 15 rebounds against USC. He and Byron have an encyclopedic grasp of basketball history and a clear understanding of the way the game is played. Handling a live crowd must be tricky, but they never falter or seem rattled.

> Joe, who has an uncanny knack for making you see the action, does the running narrative. Then Byron picks up the analysis while Joe takes a breath.

When they broadcast out-of-town games, my friend Sister Jane Roberts says she'd rather listen to them than watch it on TV. They are that good. Joe, who has an uncanny knack for making you see the action, does the running narrative. Then Byron picks up the analysis while Joe takes a breath. Byron has a tremendous relationship with the players, who respect him as one of the superstars of Xavier. He can put his finger on the team's strengths and weaknesses without hectoring or being mean spirited.

Byron Larkin and Joe Sunderman, respect and an uncanny knack.

I think he'd be a great coach, if he ever decided to give up his radio career.

About a hundred fans usually show up to hear them at the Dilly, including Chris's parents and his pretty wife, Christi, who was Christi Hester when she played guard for University of Dayton's women's basketball team from 1996 to 2000. No coach at Xavier during my time there has had a stronger family connection than Chris. I marvel at his ability to balance an intense dedication to his job with loyalty to them. His young daughters, Hailee and Lainee, are familiar figures at games and special events, and both Chris and Christi have coached their girls' teams. You just know that whatever time Chris can snatch from his schedule, he gives to his family.

Growing up in the Cincinnati suburb of North College Hill, Chris was a star at St. Xavier High School, my brother Tom's alma mater. He transferred from the University of Evansville after his sophomore year to play for Pete Gillen at Xavier, and is very popular with the hometown crowd at the Dilly, who are mostly middle-aged and older. They all seem to know each other and chew quietly during the show.

Then there is the equally true-Xavier-blue Lew Hirt Society. Not quiet, not quiet at all. My seat at Cintas Center is right in front of several of them, and they always greet me with what appears to be genuine enthusiasm. They bill themselves as extreme fans who live at least 100 miles from the statue of D'Artagnan and are named for Xavier's head basketball coach from 1946 to 1951. They glory in noting that they have many other requirements for membership, "which are secret."

The O'Malia brothers, Dave and Dan, never miss a game, driving to Cincinnati from Indianapolis, even in awful weather. Dan, who graduated from Xavier in 1969, taught high school English before taking over the family's grocery store chain. A popular motivational speaker, he was described by the *Indianapolis Business Journal* as a "customer service guru." Dave, a 1973 Xavier alum, is corporate counsel for Marsh Foods, which bought the family stores in 2001.

Funny and exuberant, the O'Malias are equal opportunity scolds, yelling at players, referees and coaches. They are never offensive—at least not to me, but then I have not been the object of their high decibel attention.

Jim Alerding, a 1967 graduate and season ticket holder since 1983, sits with them, behind me at the Cintas Center, wearing the signature blue Lew Hirt cap. "I have been a Xavier fan through thick and thin," he says, noting that after a single winning season his freshman year at Xavier, "we stunk for about fifteen years. So, now I am enjoying the thick."

All for One and the Launching Pad

A CPA with his own consulting business, he has spent a large portion of his career testifying as an expert witness in lawsuits involving business valuations and economic damages. "I've always been grateful to the Jesuits for demanding that we get a real liberal arts education at Xavier," he says. "My career was in accounting, but I sure used my minor in philosophy and the theology courses that were required. You weren't just studying for a job. You were studying for a life."

Michael Davenport calls it "being intentional." Coach Mack, back when he was director of basketball operations in 1999, put together a panel of former players to talk to student-athletes. They shared their real life experiences after basketball—finances, job interviewing, time management, what it feels like when you are no longer living your life in the midst of applause with your name up on the scoreboard.

The group included Mark Poynter, a surgeon now, who came to know several Sisters of Notre Dame when he was in undergraduate school. He was much beloved by Sister Mary Paul Peng, who remembered him years later. In the recovery room after a surgery, she fluttered her lovely epicanthic eyes, looked up at the doctor at her bedside and breathed, "Oh, good, it's the basketball player."

"I don't know how guys like Mark did it, how they kept up with their studies" Michael says. "The amount of work an athlete puts in is unbelievable. And the attention you get is not really the best preparation for the rest of your life." He says it begins in high school, maybe even junior high.

"You get a lot of attention for your ability in sports. It skews your vision of real life. You start thinking maybe basketball will be your ticket. For most of us, it was not. I had strong parents, who helped me know that I should not put all my eggs into that particular basket. You need people to bring truth into your life."

Michael Davenport met his wife, Heidy, a Montessori teacher in Cincinnati Public Schools, at Xavier. The couple has two teen-aged sons. "We go to games at Cintas, sure, but I don't know what they'll decide to do athletically. I try to tell them that sports can teach you to contribute to a team, a lesson that's great prep for a lot of things. I loved my time at Xavier. Learned a lot, met people who made a difference in my life," he says.

"I still talk to some of the guys from my team—Mark Poynter, Tyrone Hill, Byron Larkin—but we talk about what we are doing today. I would never want a kid to think at age 22 that he has just finished the best years of his life. College is a beginning, a place where you pick up tools for later." Perspective, he says, is the key. Especially about athletics.

"Xavier was a great launching pad."

Life after basketball—Maurice McAfee, his wife, Candice, and son, Samuel.

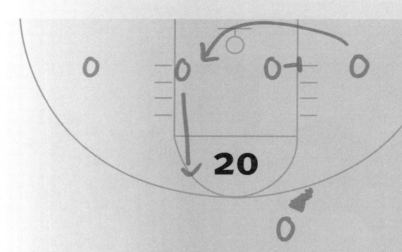

20

Family Ties and a Numbers Game

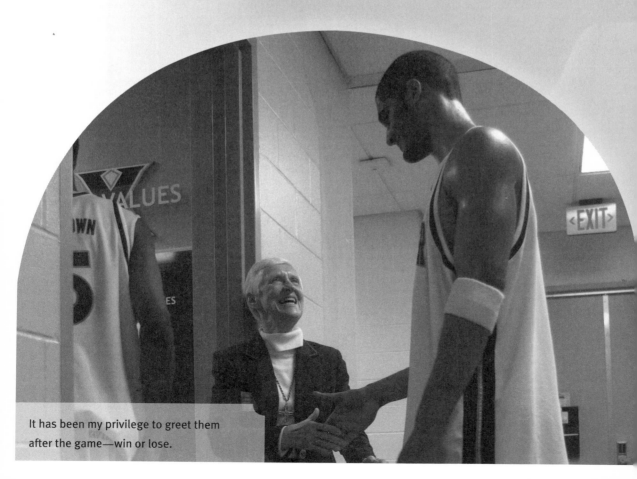

It has been my privilege to greet them after the game—win or lose.

My father and my twin brother, Tom, both CPAs, lived with numbers. And so do I. Not money, of course. My vow of poverty is quite intact. The numbers that have surrounded me are points, scores, grades, statistics, percentages. And I have learned that these numbers are not merely a record of the past but a predictor of the future.

A decade into the NCAA's academic reform, its Division I sliding scale gives athletes who have low grades in high school a chance to become eligible if they have good SAT or ACT scores. The tests supposedly predict their ability to succeed. Good test scores tell me that a student is bright, capable of learning. Good grades tell me that a student knows how to learn.

The system works as long as we understand that the student who arrives on campus with poor grades, offset by higher test scores, is likely to need a lot more help. Expensive, consistent help.

A young man I'll call Jacob was recruited from a high school plagued with high crime and low test scores. He'd never been in trouble himself and was a talented basketball player, a strong shooter. Academically, he was just keeping his head above water. He came for an unofficial visit to Xavier during his junior year of high school. As always, I talked to him about our academic standards, tried to give him a sense of what would be expected of him, how difficult it might be. He nodded solemnly. He didn't know what he didn't know. Neither did we. A year later he signed with us.

He needed every shred of help our system could provide—tutors in every subject, student assistants, summer school, learning aids, counseling. His mother lived close to the Xavier campus in an enormous old house that had been divided into small apartments. She had several other children, and Jacob went home most weekends to see his family.

Sometimes he just didn't come back.

When he started missing classes, I tried calling early Monday mornings. Somebody else would always answer—his mother, I think—and tell me Jacob was on his way. Chances were not good that he would arrive in time for his early classes. Every once in a while, I'd drive to his mother's house and park at the curb before I called. Then, if he went skidding out the door, pulling on his jacket, I could get him to campus.

Sitting there, sipping coffee one morning, waiting for the right time to punch the send button on my cell phone, I could see the building's landlord throwing a neighbor's possessions out onto the lawn as somebody was evicted. Some people on the street were up because they hadn't been to bed yet. They rummaged through the clothing and furniture at the curb, taking what they wanted. It was noisy. When Jacob complained of being tired, I believed him.

Then he started missing classes during the week, and I was furious, called him into my office. He was late and complained again about being tired. Exasperated, I barely heard him. Same old complaint, I thought. I was running late myself, heading for a luncheon where I'd agreed to speak. I told Jacob to come with me to my car, so I could walk and rant at the same time. I really was angry.

As I stalked to the parking lot, hurrying up a few steps, I looked back to see him hanging onto the stair rails, pulling himself up. Finally, I paused and stared at his face. He had been saying he didn't feel well, but I wasn't listening. He looked terrible. Alarmed, I hustled him out to my car and took him to the athletics trainer, who put him in the hospital. Some kind of flu bug had galloped out of control. He was dehydrated and very sick.

When I went to his room at University Hospital, he was hooked up to an IV and stayed there for several days. His recovery took a while, and he didn't get to play much. His coaches were trying to get him back on his feet, but he became impatient. Meanwhile, he got an offer from another, bigger university and transferred there at the end of the year. His new coach called me after school started.

"Hey," he said, "this kid is telling me that you gave him all this tutoring..." Well, I keep very complete records, if I do say so, and I recounted what we had been doing for Jacob while he was at Xavier. The coach told me that would have exhausted his budget for the whole year for all the school's athletes, including football and basketball. Jacob transferred again, this time to a Division II school. The last time I saw him, he told me he'd quit school to play basketball overseas and said he'd still like to get his degree some day. I hope he will come back to us.

Jordan Crawford is another student I'd like to see on campus again someday. I'm probably dreaming. He seems pretty happy where he is, playing NBA ball for the Golden State Warriors, which as Michael Davenport says, is like "winning the lottery with a kicker." Jordan came to Xavier as a transfer student in 2008 from Indiana University, which had been tainted by a recruiting scandal. Jordan, who was absolutely blameless in Indiana University's problems, nonetheless was ordered by the NCAA to sit out a year before he could play for us.

By this time, I think Jordan felt thoroughly cuffed around by the system. After IU's Coach Kelvin Sampson quit, Jordan played for an interim coach before Indiana hired Tom Crean. Then he came to Xavier expecting to play for Sean Miller, who left for Arizona before Jordan's year of ineligibility was up. Luckily, instead of somebody he didn't know, Coach Chris Mack took over the team for Jordan's first year with us.

During all this, Jordan was anchored by his parents. His mother, Sylvia, worked for the city of Detroit as a publicist and was involved in his life from afar, keeping tabs on his grades and his state of mind. His brother, Joe, a fine basketball player in his own right was also a force in his life. Me—not so much. He kept his head down, practiced with the team, learned to follow our study rules and finally became eligible to play in the 2009-10 season. But I never managed to get books to compete with the lure of basketball.

He led Xavier and the Atlantic 10 in scoring, our first scoring leader since Byron Larkin, then left to play with the NBA after his junior year. He played for the Atlanta Hawks, the Washington Wizards and the Boston Celtics before being traded to the Warriors in Oakland, California. In the history of the NBA draft, Jordan is the fifth former Musketeer to be selected in the first round, a list that includes David West, James Posey, Brian Grant and Tyrone Hill. Of these, he is the only one who left before his senior year. Coach Mack spent draft night at a private party for the Crawfords in Detroit, saying, "Jordan and his family will always be a part of Xavier." And he means it.

We never give up, not really. Pete Gillen found a way to get a degree for an athlete who dropped out of Xavier before the coach even arrived on campus. I saw Coach Bob Staak at an alumni reception in March of 2014. He asked me to call a couple of his guys who still do not have degrees to see if I could get them to complete their work. One is in Europe; one has disappeared. I will do so. Gladly.

In the past decade, according to NCAA records, 13,000 former student-athletes who left without graduating have returned to campuses to earn degrees. Nearly half those students competed in the high-profile sports of baseball, men's basketball, football and women's basketball. The latest figures released by the NCAA show overall improvement in each of these same sports, amid questions about academic priorities in big-time college sports and the NCAA's role in overseeing them. The governing body for college sports is facing challenges inside and outside the organization, including lawsuits and congressional hearings.

President Mike Graham says when asked about Xavier's future with the NCAA, "If you do what you're supposed to be doing—keeping sports in balance with the mission of the university—you're not really going to have much of a problem. We'll just have to figure out the details."

However all this is finally resolved, I am confident that Xavier University is well positioned. Our playbook is solid, beginning with Jeff Fogelson's admonition to me in 1986: "Education is the assignment, the top priority. Your duty is to the student, not the team." Then along came Pete Gillen who gave me the right to bench players who weren't doing well in the classroom. Long before the rules were tightened, years before rigorous NCAA scrutiny, Xavier University with its Jesuit spirituality and intellect, set out to do the right thing by its student-athletes.

> Numbers can guide our expectations, but I have seen time and time again the terrible and wonderful impact of the family.

Numbers can guide our expectations, but I have seen time and time again the terrible and wonderful impact of the family. Jacob's mother, crushed by poverty, allowed him to squander the opportunity his athletic gift afforded him. One father told me flatly that he didn't care if his son opened another book in his life: "He'll make a fortune in the NBA." On the other side of the family ledger is James Posey's dad, who took a second job to pay his son's tuition while he caught up on his studies and became eligible to play. And Michael Davenport's father used his vacation time from his job at General Motors to travel from Michigan to his son's games. What if Tyrone Hill's grandmother hadn't taken him to church on Sundays?

Brandon Cole's grandmother, Diane Flowers, wrote to me for Mother's Day: "I can't help but want to honor you for the years spent 'mothering' so many young men through the door of XU. It always was reassuring to us mothers and grandmothers knowing that you were there in our absence." Well, I believe that those mothers and grandmothers, in many instances, paved the way for me to work with their children. They taught them to trust and to respect women.

Sean Miller and I both worked with a young man Coach Miller describes as "rough around the edges." He played ball and he graduated, but he continues to flounder, bouncing from job to job with a young son who captures his attention only occasionally. I still am not sure what will become of him, but I know he stands a better chance of righting himself than he would have without his Xavier experiences. Another young man has dropped from sight, lost touch with his teammates, returned to the crime-riddled neighborhood of his youth.

One of my greatest challenges as a teacher and as a member of the support team for our students is figuring out the formula to get them ready to succeed on their own, when I am not there to pound on the door, when a manager is not going to hand them clean socks, when a coach is not there to tell them when to run drills and when to sleep. Four years at a university, two hours a day at a study table, lessons from talented teachers and coaches—in the grand scheme of things, it's not a lot of time. Much is made of our record of graduating all our senior basketball players, but that is only the beginning.

The day they get their diploma is called Commencement for a reason. As Michael Davenport says, Xavier is a launching pad, an incubator, not a final destination. Father Hoff wanted "everything" for Xavier University. And I have always wanted "everything" for Xavier's student-athletes. Grades. Sports. And more. I want them to leave with a curiosity for the world, a taste of the satisfaction of service to others.

> "I want them to leave with a curiosity for the world, a taste of the satisfaction of service to others."

As I look back at my heartfelt but unformed spiritual conversion in high school on the weekend of the socks that were never knit, I am grateful anew to my father, who knew me better than I thought, insisting that I postpone my entry into the convent. "Patience is the companion of wisdom," St. Augustine wrote.

At Mount St. Joseph, my impatient aspirations as a religious were steeped in a classic education and forged by centuries of wisdom. Would my rebellious nature have accepted the cornbread and the endless scrubbing of woodwork at the convent without the lessons I learned from St. Thomas Aquinas, from the Aeneid?

When I read Virgil's Neque ignorare mala miseris succurrere disco—"Not being ignorant of bad things, I learn to help the wretched."—were these seeds of my eventual service through the law?

Did contemplating the words of Aquinas spark my determination to urge athletes to become life-long students, to challenge themselves through service to others? The things that we love tell us who we are. And give me the courage to take them into my heart knowing their lives with me are temporary? "If the highest aim of a captain were to preserve his ship, he would keep it in port forever."

I developed my habit of rising early in college—before the rest of the world drew me to it. My surroundings were quiet, bucolic. I was, as Richie Harris would say years later, taking time to learn, making sense of my life, learning to think. Reading Augustine's *City of God* and the *Aeneid* of Virgil in Latin forced me onto a measured, contemplative path, coming to a deeper, intellectual understanding of my spiritual choice. I wrestled with the ancient notions of the sacraments and God's love and my own desire to help others. The Church teaches that what is received is received according to the disposition of the receiver: ex opere operantis. The sacraments are signs of grace, but the grace only works in us to the extent that we are open to it.

I keep that connection with Christ in my life in many ways, not the least of which is avid attendance at Mass, wherever I am. One of the first things I do when I'm on the road with one of our teams is to find the nearest Catholic church. My legal work for the poor has opened another avenue for me to serve, and I am sure I am meant to do this work. On the day of my very first trial, I walked down the broad empty corridor at the Hamilton County Courthouse in late afternoon, my heels clicking on the marble floor, grateful to have won the case for a very needy man. I suddenly felt God take my hand. He was with me, confirmation that this is right, a good thing for me to do.

What was this? St. Thomas Aquinas might say, "To one who has faith, no explanation is necessary. To one without faith, no explanation is possible."

The latest strategic plan for Xavier athletics, through the year 2019 is centered by Magis, a Latin word that means "doing more" or "doing better," taken from Ad Majorem Dei Gloriam, meaning "for the greater glory of God." It's the philosophy of doing more, for Christ, and therefore for others. It is a Jesuit ideal to promote continuous growth and improvement. Father Graham calls it "forming men and women for others."

When I hear of David West stepping forward to help families after the Katrina disaster in New Orleans and bringing books of poetry into the Pacers locker room, I am confident that his time at Xavier contributed to the kind of person he became. When Brian Grant bends over the bed of a sick child, who is not his own, I believe that his natural kindness and compassion were nurtured at this institution.

People describe me as relentless, and I think I am relentlessly upbeat—supported over a lifetime by my faith and my family. What might have happened to me if my own father had given up on his unruly, grieving girl child? What if our dear Aunt Mary had not put her own life on hold to ride herd on her brother's two motherless children? I vaguely remember how excited Aunt Mary had been when women began to leave the home to work in factories during World War II, but just then she was asked to take care of Tom and me. Did she have dreams of being Rosie the Riveter? We would never know. Duty came first.

Family Ties and a Numbers Game

Sister Thomas Mary with nephew, Daniel, future Ohio High School Coach of the Year.

Even before that time, I believe that my mother—who took my side against authority, who allowed me to gallop around a field on a thousand-pound animal which scared her to death, who set an example of service to others—put my life's course in motion. Tom and Theresa's five children and their children are integral to my sense of well being. When the children were little, my brother and his wife took a rare vacation, asking Sister Jane Roberts and me to look after them for a week.

"Every time I walked into a room, you were praying," my niece Molly Fleming teased.

"Five children under the age of 10," I retorted. "We were praying for your parents' safe return." We have a relationship like none other in my life. No one teases me like my nephew, Daniel, and no one loves me like my brother, Tom. The walls of Tom and Theresa's home are covered with photographs and mementos of lives well lived, First Communions, weddings, holidays. A story in the *Cincinnati Enquirer* by columnist Paul Daugherty holds a place of honor. It's about my brother Tom and Daniel, a high school basketball coach in Cincinnati for more than twenty years, a Father's Day story about Tom's constant and loving support.

Did Tom's weekly letters to me during my days as a postulant matter? You bet. I treasure the memory of Tom and Theresa making me part of their wedding, bringing the celebration to me at The Summit chapel. My father, often stern when I was a youngster and certainly doubtful about my vocation at first, was a complete softie with his grandchildren. Christmas turkey, shamrocks sent from Ireland each year by family there in time for St. Patrick's Day—these things have sustained me in large and small ways.

My niece, Mary Miller, came to me with questions before she chose a college, then asked again twenty years later when her daughter was wrestling with education choices. "Good advice, gently given," Mary told a friend. "Plus, I'm always impressed that Aunt Rose Ann is so up-to-date. I think she was the first one in our family to learn how to text. But, of course, she always found ways to communicate with her students. Amazing. She's amazing, and she has always been there for me."

My family has "been there for me" as well. I remember when I had to move to a place that wouldn't allow my little Schnauzer, a present from Dad after I got my Ph.D from Miami. I asked Tom and Theresa if they would adopt him. My nephew, Kevin, who lives in San Francisco, still howls with laughter when he remembers the exchange. "We asked the name of the dog when we picked him up. Sir Lancelot of Bellwood and Beaucrest. Classic. So precise. We called him Lance."

Michael, who lives in Seattle, says I became infinitely more interesting to him as a teenager when I began rubbing shoulders with Xavier's basketball players.

"No matter how many communes anybody invents," Margaret Mead said, "the family always creeps back." Michael Davenport says he was surrounded by people who were convinced of his worth off the basketball court, "my mom, my grandmother, my dad, my wife—people who brought truth into my life." My blood ties have been reinforced and strengthened by my religious family, my Summit family, my Trinity family and my Xavier family.

These families pop back into my life with soothing regularity, reassuring me that they may leave but I will not lose them. Not really.

When I vacate my seat in the Cintas Center arena at the two-minute mark, it is not because I think the game is finished, not because I know who will win and who will lose. I simply don't want to miss the opportunity to be waiting at the locker room door for the young people who contribute so much to Xavier University and so much to my life. I want to be there to pray with the team, something they do after every game. At that moment, the score does not matter. Something more profound, more mysterious than numbers, holds sway over us.

Sister Teresa Mary McCarthy, the teacher at The Summit who found me interesting, happened upon me sixty years ago, scrubbing baseboards at the novitiate, my head down, wearing my dark blue work apron over my black habit. "Don't take any of this too seriously," she advised me, waving her hand at the polished floor, the scrubbed wood. I knew what she meant. Life would offer more profound work if I was ready, if I had the grace to accept.

Wherever you see a need, I have learned, that's where God is calling you. So, I firmly believe the game is not over for me. Perhaps the most glorious moments are yet to come.

Epilogue

*T*he traffic jam starts early, radiating from homes and hotels toward Xavier University and the solid bulk of its Cintas Center. No ESPN satellite truck. No body paint. No blue fright wigs. The cameras are mostly iPods, the images quick selfies.

Gridlock on the brisk spring morning of graduation day is cheerful, polite. Turn signals engaged. Horns mute. An occasional car door pops open to spew a scout, quick-stepping to save seats, the rest of the convoy continuing on to find parking for Commencement, the Main Event. The spotlight will be on 747 students who arrived earlier, clutching cards with seat row and position in the processional, shepherded by staff with crackling walkie-talkies.

Inside, the arena is transformed to fulfill the promise made by the men who dreamed it there, the place that basketball built.

No shriek of rubber soles against hardwood. The maple floor, in four-by-eight-foot sections, has been stripped down to the concrete base, picked up, racked and stored under the Joseph Club. Building services manager Max Kappel's crew, unseen, takes pride in preparing the vast space, says Max, "for the most important day of the year." A 2009 Xavier MBA, he loves the physical analogy of the transition.

Chairs in precise rows replace free throw lanes and looping three-point arcs. The sound system's throb is side-lined by Edward Elgar's *Pomp and Circumstance*, cadence for a sedate processional of peep-toed shoes and loafers. A Xavier-blue river of tasseled caps and gowns is embellished by colors of honors and academic status. The center-hung scoreboard displays the names of graduates and sees them across the stage. Game scores and sponsor messages are blotted out by bright lights proclaiming: Service rooted in justice and love.

Big East university banners have been replaced by flags from the countries of origin for this year's graduates—fifteen of them, lined up alphabetically next to the Stars and Stripes, from the Bahamas to Vietnam. Numbers, scores, of course, have been kept. Michael Petrany of Huntington, West Virginia, who worked his way through philosophy, biology, chemistry and German to emerge with a 4.0, was singled out for service and academic achievement.

Speaker Matthew Kelly challenged honorees to "take the long view," underscored by Walter Bunker, age 90, a World War II veteran winning his degree after seventy years' study, off and on. Charlie Gallagher was recognized for his boundless generosity, as his grandchildren watched from Presidential Suite 313, squinting at the stage far below. "Is PaPa still smiling and looking all handsome?" His wife, Diane, answers promptly, "He is."

Jeff Eschmeyer records his wife, Debra, as she accepts the Magis Award for feeding the hungry, a theme recognized in an exhortation from Father Peter-Hans Kolvenbach, Superior General Emeritus of the Society of Jesus, in the preface of the day's elaborately printed program of events:

"How can a booming economy, the most prosperous and global ever, still leave over half of humanity in poverty? Injustice is rooted in a spiritual problem, and its solution requires a spiritual conversion of each one's heart..."

Many people in this vast space, myself included, believe the solution could come from the young people here today collecting handshakes, hugs and the occasional fist-bump from an exuberant President Michael Graham. I am seated on the stage behind him, across from my game night place in the stands. As I receive the Paul L. O'Connor, S.J., Leadership Award, I wish I could split the handsome plaque into fragments to share with faculty and coaches who have been with me all these years.

During two and a half hours while undergraduates troop forward to become official alumni, I have plenty of time to reflect. Charlie Gallagher has been presented with the Leadership Medallion Award, which hereafter will be named in his honor. A 1960 graduate, Charlie went to school here when it was a men's commuter school. Now, the class of 2017 comes to us from forty states, the District of Columbia and twenty-one foreign countries. Nearly 56 percent of them are female and 54 percent of them are from outside Ohio.

Many people, again myself included, believe that our scholarly institution often comes to the attention of prospective customers as a result of the success of our men's basketball team.

Although I know to expect it, I am startled when the boom of a mock cannon blasts a shower of confetti and streamers over the crowd of newly confirmed graduates. We exit the arena down hallways lined with portraits of basketball players from Xavier's past. Michael, Byron, Tyrone, Jimmy, Derek, Tu, Dante, Richie, Jamie, Brian, Brandon, David, Jamal—and dozens of others who worked so hard to play their best game here, often finding new purpose and "spiritual conversion of the heart" along the way. I believe people who love this university, where tradition and loyalty are treasured, will not forget the gladiators in baggy tunics and shorts who helped make this day possible.

I never will.

Index